# GOD.COM 2
Inspirational Impact

# GOD.COM 2

## Inspirational Impact

Compiled and Edited by
**Albert A. C. Waite** PhD

MANDRA PUBLISHING

First published in 2004 by
Mandra Publishing
P.O. Box 5136
Riseley
RG7 1GT


Copyright © 2004 Albert A C Waite


ISBN 0 540429 5 6


A catalogue record for this book is available from the
British Library.

Printed and bound in Great Britain by
The Cromwell Press Ltd
Trowbridge
Wiltshire

This book is dedicated to all who bought
GOD.COM volume one

# BENEFICIARY

Part of the profit from this book will be donated to good causes. We had hoped to identify specific support for a Caribbean senior citizens home in West London, but we had to go to press before the committee made their decision. Mandra Publishing will continue to support good causes. So far we have supported a church development programme, two church building funds, a Sickle Cell society and a Basic school in the Caribbean.

We thank you for buying this book, which help us to help others.

www.mandrapublishing.com

# ACKNOWLEDGEMENTS

They are still arriving: stories, poems, prayers and thoughts. Every day they come. They come with the same specific message: 'Share this with as many people as you can.'

There are still many people who are not connected to the internet. How would they know of these masterpieces without GOD.COM 2? Even those who have the internet say, "It is good to have them in a book."

Humongous thanks again to all those internet wizards who keep sharing the pearls they receive with me. Some regularly: Blossom Thomas, Simeon Esson, Annette Roberts, Claudette Coleman, Beulah Jarrett, Colin Samuels; and others less frequently: Hanna Baisden, Jackie Johnson, Joseph Barrett, Glenda Waite-Drummond, Sharleen Wilson, and Bernice Charles. There are also those whose names I forgot to save. All e-contributions are valued equally.

Much appreciation is due to Alicia A C Waite, my assistant editor, and to all readers of the first GOD.COM, to whom this book is dedicated. To Greg Wilson, whose patience gives us the cover of this volume.

And finally, but most significantly, to the known God, who inspired all the unknown authors, who unselfishly send out their work on the internet.

THANK YOU

# CONTENTS

11

## PRAYERS

## POEMS

## WORDS TO LIVE BY

# FROM THE EDITOR...

As with the first GOD.COM, this new volume is a compilation of stories, poems, prayers and thoughts (words to live by) that convey a profound message to the heart, in a simple but powerful way.

GOD.COM 2 finds its roots in the overwhelming success and the many positive comments from every age group who read the first GOD.COM. As before, we have made changes in the body of the texts and added new titles in most cases, to give that extra appeal to the growing readership of what is becoming a GOD.COM series. We are aware that less than 2% of the world's population owns a computer so we have complied with the requests to share the e-mails received, by making these heart-tugging 'gems' available in a book.

We know that this bigger and even more inspirational and motivational compilation, GOD.COM 2, will encourage every reader in any situation to seek and appreciate God, the Creator of the Universe, who gives each of us *free will*, to work His purpose out in our lives if we will only let Him.

There is no doubt that the authors, mostly unknown, of the contents of GOD.COM 2, allowed the Holy Spirit to inspire their work for our benefit. We believe that you too will want to share GOD.COM 2 with your friends, in the same way thousands shared the first GOD.COM.

Sit back and enjoy what you are about to discover.

AACW
*Conifers*
*Three Mile Cross*
*October 2004*

# GOD SEARCHING FOR YOU

To Whom It May Concern...

I heard you were considering a new manager in your life. I would like to apply for the job as I believe I am the qualified candidate. I created the heavens and the earth. I AM.

I am the only one that has ever done this job successfully. I was the first manager of human beings. In fact, I made them. So, naturally, I know how humanity works and what is best to get people back into proper working condition. It will be like having the manufacturer as your personal mechanic.

If this is your first time considering Me, I would like to point out that My salary has already been paid by the blood of My Son, Jesus, on the cross of Calvary. What I need from you is the acknowledgment that the price is sufficient to pay for all of your sins and your independence from Me.

I need you to believe this in your heart and to *tell* somebody else about your decision. The next thing I ask is the right to change and fix your life so you can learn how to stay close to Me. I will make some major changes and revisions. They are not for you to worry about.

I need your permission to execute these changes: in My way and in My time. I will change your desires and give you the *strength* to make the changes. Please keep your hands out of the way. I won't require assistance. Don't try to help me and don't resist me. I really do need your full commitment and cooperation. If you give me those, the process can go smoothly without delays.
I look forward to hearing from you.

Sincerely Yours,

God

PS. My resume is on page 217

# STORIES

# SOMEONE UNDERSTANDS

A farmer had some puppies he needed to sell. He painted a sign advertising the 20 pups and set about nailing it to a post at the edge of his yard. As he was driving the last nail into the post, he felt a tug on his overalls, and he looked down into the eyes of a little boy.

"Mister," he said, "I want to buy one of your puppies."

"Well," said the farmer, as he wiped the sweat off his forehead, "These puppies come from fine parents and cost a good deal of money."

The boy dropped his head for a moment. Then, reaching deep into his pocket, he pulled out a handful of change and held it up to the farmer. "I've got thirty-nine pence. Is that enough to take a look?"

"Sure," said the farmer. And with that he let out a whistle. "Here, Dolly!" he called. Out from the doghouse and down the ramp ran Dolly followed by four little balls of fur. The little boy pressed his face against the chain link fence, his eyes dancing with delight.

But, as the dogs made their way to the fence, the little boy noticed something else stirring inside the doghouse. Slowly, another little ball appeared, this one noticeably smaller. Down the ramp it slid, then in a somewhat awkward manner, the little pup began hobbling toward the others, doing its best to catch up.

"I want that one," the little boy said, pointing to the runt.

The farmer knelt down at the boy's side and said, "Son, you don't want that puppy. He will never be able to run and play with you like these other dogs would."

With that the little boy stepped back from the fence, reached down and began rolling up one leg of his trousers. In doing so he revealed a steel brace running down both sides of his leg, attached to a specially made shoe.

Looking back up at the farmer, he said, "You see sir, I don't run too well myself, and he will need someone who understands."

The world is full of people who need someone who understands.

Jesus understands because He's been there before us.

*For we do not have a High Priest who cannot sympathise with our weaknesses, but was in all points tempted as we are, yet without sin. Let us therefore come boldly to the throne of grace that we may obtain mercy and find grace to help in time of need (Hebrews 4:15, 16).*

# MY ROOM

In that place between wakefulness and dreams, I found myself in a room. There were no distinguishing features except for one wall covered with small index cards files. They were like the ones in libraries that list titles by author or subject in alphabetical order. But these files, which stretched from floor to ceiling and seemingly endlessly in either direction, had very different headings.

As I drew near the wall of files, the first to catch my attention was one that reads, "Girls I Have Liked." I opened it and began flipping through the cards. I quickly shut it, shocked to realize that I recognized the names written on each one. And then without being told, I knew exactly where I was. This lifeless room with its small files was a crude catalogue system for my life.

Here were written the actions of my every moment, big and small, in a detail my memory couldn't match. A sense of wonder and curiosity, coupled with horror, stirred within me as I began randomly opening files and exploring their content. Some brought joy and sweet memories; others a sense of shame and regret so intense that I would look over my shoulder to see if anyone was watching.

A file named "Friends" was next to one marked "Friends I Have Betrayed." The titles ranged from the mundane to the outright weird. "Books I Have Read," "Lies I Have Told," "Comfort I Have Given," "Jokes I Have Laughed At." Some were almost hilarious in their exactness: "Things I've Yelled at My Brothers". Others I couldn't laugh at: "Things I Have Done in My Anger", "Things I Have Muttered Under My Breath at My Parents." I never ceased to be surprised by the contents.

Often there were many more cards than I expected in some file drawers. Sometimes fewer than I hoped. The sheer volume of the life I had lived overwhelmed me. Could it be possible that I had the time in my 20 years to write each of these thousands or even millions of cards? But each card confirmed this truth. Each was written in my own handwriting. Each signed with my signature.

When I pulled out the file marked "Songs I Have Listened to," I realised how the files grew to contain their contents. The cards were packed tightly, and yet after two or three yards, I hadn't found the end of the file. I shut it, shamed, not so much by the quality of music, but more by the vast amount of time I knew that file represented.

When I came to a file marked "Lustful Thoughts," I felt a chill run through my body. I pulled the file out only an inch, not willing to test its size, and drew out a card. I shuddered at its detailed content. I felt sick to think that such a moment had been recorded. An almost animal rage broke on me.

One thought dominated my mind: "No one must ever see these cards! No one must ever see this room! I have to destroy them!" In an insane frenzy I yanked the file out. Its size didn't matter now. I had to empty it and burn the cards. But as I took it at one end and began pounding it on the floor, I could not dislodge a single card. I became desperate and pulled out a card, only to find it as strong as steel when I tried to tear it. Defeated and utterly helpless, I returned the file to its slot. Leaning my forehead against the wall, I let out a long, self-pitying sigh. And then I saw it. The title read: "People I Have Shared the Gospel With." The handle was brighter than those around it, newer, almost unused. I pulled on its handle and a small box not more than three inches long fell into my hands. I could count the cards it contained on one hand.

And then the tears came. I began to weep. Sobs so deep that the hurt started in my stomach and shook through me. I fell on my knees and cried: I cried out of shame - from the overwhelming shame of it all. The rows of file shelves swirled in my tear-filled eyes. No one must ever know of this room. I must lock it up and hide the key.

But then as I brushed away the tears, I saw Him.
No, please not Him. Not here. Oh, anyone but
Jesus. I watched helplessly as He began to open
the files and read the cards. I couldn't bear to
watch His response. And in the moments I could
bring myself to look at His face, I saw a sorrow
deeper than my own. He seemed to intuitively
go to the worst boxes. Why did He have to read
every one?

Finally, He turned and looked at me from across
the room. He looked at me with pity in His eyes.
But this was a pity that didn't anger me. I
dropped my head, covered my face with my
hands and began to cry again. He walked over
and put His arm around me. He could have said
so many things. But He didn't say a word - He
just cried with me.

Then He got up and walked back to the wall of
files. Starting at one end of the room, He took
out a file and, one by one, began to sign His
name over mine on each card. "No!" I shouted,
rushing to Him. All I could find to say was "No,
no," as I pulled the card from Him. His name
shouldn't be on these cards. But there it was,
written in red, so rich, so dark and so alive. The
name of Jesus covered mine. It was written with
His blood. He gently took the card back. He
smiled a sad smile and began to sign some
more cards.

I don't think I'll ever understand how He did it so quickly, but the next instant it seemed I heard Him close the last file and walk back to my side. He placed His hand on my shoulder and said, "It is finished."

I stood up and He led me out of the room. There was no lock on its door. There were more cards to be written....

\*\*\*

*I can do all things through Christ who strengthens me (Philippians 4:13).*

*For God so loved the world that He gave His only Son, that whoever believes in Him shall not perish but have eternal life. (John 3:16)*

*Story by Brian Moore*
*(Written at aged 17, now deceased)*

# LORD, SEND ME

The Master called my name one day because He needed someone to go on errands for Him.

I said, "Lord, in my spare time, between school, between spending time with my husband, working from eight to six, and trying to coordinate a programme for my community to help our children do better. I'll help you Lord but look, I can't go right now, because I have so much to do."

He said, "Well where shall I find such a person? I thought I saw your name on my list of available people."
"Well, Lord, that was the prayer that I prayed last year, but since then, things have changed."

He said, "Like what?"
"Well, I'm working on my PhD and I'm needed by so many people and my husband is always wanting something done. And on top of that, my community expects me to help and give to them. So...."

"Well, since you're busy, I'll let you go. But we'll talk again, if you have some time."

I went on through the days and the weeks and the months, completing my tasks as always. But one evening, while preparing for exams, I received a call from the hospital concerning my husband. He had been in a terrible accident and was in a critical condition. I dropped everything and ran to the hospital, where I found my husband hanging on for dear life. I immediately begin to pray: "Lord, don't take him now, I can't bear it," but my prayer seemed to echo off the wall and return into my own ears.

The next morning, I left the hospital tired and reached the university just in time to begin my exams. As the professors began asking me questions, I opened my mouth to speak, but nothing came out. In my mind, I began praying, praying hard, but my prayer echoed again and I found myself upset at the Lord because He was nowhere to be found.

I could not explain to them what was happening. After leaving from my exams, I called in to work because I was so distraught at all that was going on. I explained to my supervisor what had happened and she demanded that I take some time off.

After visiting my husband in the hospital that evening, I went home and fell into a sunken state, crying and despairing. Just then, I heard someone calling my name.

"Lord, is that you?"

"Well, yes it is. Do you have some time? I wanted to see if we could talk."

Instead of waiting to hear His questions, I lashed out in anger and resentment. "Why is it that? When I needed you today you couldn't be found, and last night I cried and cried, but all I heard were echoes from the walls. My husband is dying, I'm flunking my exams, I may not have a job, and you can just sit there and say you want to talk!"

The Lord interrupted me in my foolish speaking. "My child, I was busy, out looking for someone to go and tell others about me when you cried. By the time I came to answer, you had moved on to something else. So, I decided to let your husband rest, and keep you home for a few days. That way, maybe you would get in touch with me, if you had some time. You see, before your husband, the community or your job needs you, I need you. And if all these things take you away from Me, I have to almost take them away from you in order to get a moment."

I calmed down and began to cry. For I remembered my prayer of wanting to go and do for the Lord. He said, "I just wanted to check with you to see if you knew of anyone that I could send to be a witness for me and tell others about me, anyone at all?" With tears in my eyes and feeling so unworthy I said, "Lord, send me. I'll go."

\*\*\*

The Lord should never have to ask us if we have some time. When He died on the cross, He put aside everything to ensure us eternal life. We should be more than grateful to do service for the Lord, to witness and to tell anyone we can about Jesus. Don't let things in your life, whatever they may be, get you so tied up that the Lord has to become a meeting time in your yearly planner. He had more than enough time for us. The least we can do is have time for Him.

# WELCOME - MAY I JOIN YOU?

His name was Bill. He had wild hair, wears a T-shirt with holes in it, jeans and no shoes. This was literally his wardrobe for his entire four years of college. He was brilliant, kind of eccentric and very, very bright. Bill became a Christian while attending college.

Across the street from the campus was a well-dressed, very conservative church. They wanted to develop a ministry to the students, but weren't sure how to go about it. One day, Bill decided to go there.

He walked in with no shoes and wild hair, wearing jeans and a T-shirt. The service had already started, so Bill started down the aisle looking for a seat. The church was completely packed and he couldn't find a seat anywhere. By now, people were looking a bit uncomfortable, although no one said anything. Bill got closer and closer to the pulpit, and when he realised there were no seats, he just sat down on the carpet. Although perfectly acceptable behaviour at a college fellowship, trust me, this had never happened in this church before!

By now, the people were really uptight and the tension in the air was thick. The minister noticed that from way at the back of the church, a deacon was slowly making his way to the front of the church toward Bill.

This deacon was in his eighties, had grey hair, and always wore a three-piece suit. He was a godly man, elegant and dignified. He walked with a cane and, as he started walking toward this boy, everyone started saying to themselves that you couldn't blame him for what he was going to do. How can you expect a man of his age and of his background to accept some university student sitting on the floor?

It took a long time for the man to reach the boy; the church was totally silent except for the clicking of the man's cane. All eyes were focused on him. You could even hear everyone breathing. The minister had stopped preaching so the deacon could do what he had to do.

At last he reached the front of the church and the congregation watched as they saw this elderly man drop his cane on the floor. With great difficulty, he lowered himself and sat down next to Bill so that he wouldn't be alone.

When the minister gained his composure, he said, "What I'm about to preach, you will never remember. What you have just seen, you will never forget."

Be careful how you live. You may be the only 'Bible' some people will ever read.

*For man looks on the outward appearance but God knows the heart (1 Samuel 16:7).*

# THE BLESSINGS OF LIFE

Robert Matthews from Norfolk, Virginia, called a local radio station to share this on Sept 11th, 2003. He said:

A few weeks before Sept 11th, my wife and I found out we were going to have our first child. She planned a trip out to California to visit her sister.

On our way to the airport, we prayed that God would grant my wife a safe trip and be with her. Shortly after I said 'amen,' we both heard a loud pop and the car shook violently. We had blown out a tire. I replaced the tire as quickly as I could, but we still missed her flight. Both very upset, we drove home. I received a call from my father who was a retired fireman. He asked what my wife's flight number was; I explained that we missed the flight.

My father informed me that her flight was the one that crashed into the southern tower. I was too shocked to speak. My father also had more news for me; he was going to help. 'This is not something I can just sit by for, I have to do something.' I was concerned for his safety, of course, but more because he had never given his life to Christ. After a brief debate, I knew his mind was made up. Before he got off the phone, he said, 'Take good care of my grandchild.'

Those were the last words I ever heard my father say, he died while helping in the rescue effort. My joy that my prayer of safety for my wife had been answered quickly became anger.

Anger at God, at my father and at myself. I had gone for nearly two years blaming God for taking my father away. My son would never know his grandfather. To my knowledge, my father had never accepted Christ, and I never got to say goodbye. Then something happened.

About two months ago (July 2003), I was sitting at home with my wife and my son, when there was a knock on the door. I looked at my wife, but I could tell she wasn't expecting anyone. I opened the door to a couple with a small child. The man looked at me and asked if my father's name was Jake Matthews. I told him it was. He quickly grabbed my hand and said, 'I never got the chance to meet your father, but it is an honour to meet his son.' He explained to me that his wife had worked in the World Trade Centre and had been caught inside after the attack. She was pregnant and had been caught under debris.

He then explained that my father had been the one to find his wife and free her. My eyes welled up with tears as I thought of my father giving his life for people like this. He then said, 'There is something else you need to know.' His wife then told me that as my father worked to free her, she talked to him and he accepted Christ. I began sobbing at the good news. I now know that when I get to heaven, my father will be there, and that this family will be able to thank him themselves.

When their baby boy was born, they named him Jacob Matthew in honour of the man who gave his life so mother and baby could live.

***

This story should help us to realise that God is always in control. We may not see the reason behind things, and we may never understand why this side of heaven, but God is always in control.

# THE OTHER SIDE

A sick man turned to his doctor as he was preparing to leave the examination room and said, "Doctor, I am afraid to die. Tell me what lies on the other side."

Quietly the doctor replied, "I don't know."

"You don't know? You, a Christian man, do not know what is on the other side?"

The doctor was holding the handle of the door, on the other side of which came a sound of scratching and whining, and as he opened the door, a dog sprang into the room and leaped on him with an eager show of gladness.

Turning to the patient, the doctor said, "Did you notice my dog? He's never been in this room before. He didn't know what was inside. He knew nothing except that his master was here, and when the door opened, he sprang in without fear. I know little of what is on the other side of death, but I do know one thing: I know my Master is there and that is enough."

# THE BRICK

A young and successful executive was travelling down a neighbourhood street, going a bit too fast in his new Jaguar.

He was watching for kids darting out from between parked cars and slowed down when he thought he saw something.

As his car passed, no children appeared. Instead, a brick smashed into the Jag's side door!

He slammed on the brakes and backed the Jag back to the spot where the brick had been thrown. The angry driver then jumped out of the car, grabbed the nearest kid and pushed him up against a parked car shouting, "What was that all about and who are you? Just what the heck are you doing? That's a new car and that brick you threw is going to cost a lot of money. Why did you do it?"

The young boy was apologetic. "Please, mister, please. I'm sorry but I didn't know what else to do," he pleaded. "I threw the brick because no one else would stop."

With tears running down his face and off his chin, the youth pointed to a spot just around a parked car. "It's my brother," he said. "He rolled off the curb and fell out of his wheelchair and I can't lift him up."

Now sobbing, the boy asked the stunned executive, "Would you please help me get him back into his wheelchair? He's hurt and he's too heavy for me."

Moved beyond words, the driver tried to swallow the rapidly swelling lump in his throat. He hurriedly lifted the handicapped boy back into the wheelchair, then took out a handkerchief and dabbed at the fresh scrapes and cuts. A quick look told him everything was going to be okay.

"Thank you and may God bless you," the grateful child told the stranger.

Too shook up for words, the man simply watched the boy push his wheelchair-bound brother down the pavement toward their home.

It was a long, slow walk back to the Jaguar. The damage was very noticeable, but the driver never bothered to repair the dented side door. He kept the dent there to remind him of this message: Don't go through life so fast that someone has to throw a brick at you to get your attention!

God whispers in our souls and speaks to our hearts. Sometimes when we don't have time to listen, He has to throw a brick at us. It's our choice to listen or not.

# HE'S NOT HEAVY ... HE'S MY BROTHER

*Carry each other's burdens, and in this way you will fulfil the law of Christ  (Galatians 6:2, NIV).*

Sadhu Sundar Singh and a companion were travelling through a pass, high in the Himalayan Mountains. At one point, they came across a body lying in the snow.

Sundar Singh wanted to stop and help the unfortunate man, but his companion refused to stop, saying, 'We shall lose our lives if we burden ourselves with him.'

But Sundar Singh would not think of leaving the man to die in the ice and snow. As his companion bade his farewell, Sundar Singh lifted the poor traveller onto his back. With great exertion on his part, he bore the man onward, but gradually the heat from Singh's body began to warm up the beleaguered frozen fellow and he revived. Soon, both men were walking side by side. When they caught up with his former companion, they found him dead - frozen by the cold.

In the case of Sundar Singh, he was willing to lose his life on behalf of another, and in the process, found it; but in the case of his companion who sought only his own well being, he only lost it.

As a song writer later expressed it, "He ain't heavy, he's my brother." When we treat a needy person who crosses our path as our brother or sister, the rewards of carrying them until they can get on their own two feet, will far outweigh the burden of the load.

\*\*\*

*Dear God, please help me to treat each person you bring into my life as a brother or sister and be willing to help them when they need a helping hand, to help lift their spirit when they need an encouraging word, and to help carry their load when it is too heavy for them to bear alone - as you have done for me. Thank you for hearing and answering my prayer.*

*Amen.*

# CONTRADICTIONS – BUT REMEMBER

[George Carlin, the often coarse and mouthy comedian of the 70's and 80's - wrote this very eloquent, and so very appropriate post 9-11 piece, soon after his wife died]

"The paradox of our time in history is that we have taller buildings but shorter tempers, wider freeways, but narrower viewpoints.

We spend more, but have less; we buy more, but enjoy less.
We have bigger houses and smaller families; more conveniences, but less time.

We have more degrees, but less sense; more knowledge, but less judgment; more experts, yet more problems; more medicine, but less wellness.

We drink too much, smoke too much, spend too recklessly, laugh too little, drive too fast, get too angry, stay up too late, get up too tired, read too little, watch TV too much, and pray too seldom.

We have multiplied our possessions, but reduced our values.
We talk too much, love too seldom, and hate too often.

We've learned how to make a living, but not a life.
We've added years to life, not life to years.

We've been all the way to the moon and back, but have trouble crossing the street to meet a new neighbour.
We conquered outer space but not inner space.

We've done larger things, but not better things.

We've cleaned up the air, but polluted the soul.
We've conquered the atom, but not our prejudice.

We write more, but learn less.
We plan more, but accomplish less.
We've learned to rush, but not to wait.

We build more computers to hold more information, to produce more copies than ever, but we communicate less and less.

These are the times of fast foods and slow digestion, big men and small character, steep profits and shallow relationships.

These are the days of two incomes but more divorce, fancier houses, but broken homes.
These are days of quick trips, disposable diapers, throwaway morality, one night stands, overweight bodies, and pills that do everything from cheer, to quiet, to kill.

It is a time when there is much in the showroom window and nothing in the stockroom.

Remember to spend some time with your loved ones, because they are not going to be around forever.

Remember to say a kind word to someone who looks up to you in awe, because that little person soon will grow up and leave your side.

Remember to give a warm hug to the one next to you, because that is the only treasure you can give with your heart and it doesn't cost a penny.

Remember, to say, "I love you" to your partner and your loved ones, and most of all, mean it. A kiss and an embrace will mend hurt when it comes from deep inside of you.

Remember to hold hands and cherish the moment, for someday that person will not be there again.

Give time to love, give time to speak, and give time to share the precious thoughts in your mind.

Life is not measured by the number of breaths we take, but by the moments that take our breath away.

# I SHALL NOT PASS THIS WAY AGAIN

I sat with two friends, in the picture window of a quaint restaurant just off the corner of the town's square. The food and the company were both especially good that day. As we talked, my attention was drawn outside, across the street. There, walking into town, was a man who appeared to be carrying all his worldly goods on his back. He was carrying, a well-worn sign that reads, "I will work for food." My heart sank. I brought him to the attention of my friends and noticed that others around us had stopped eating to focus on him. Heads moved in a mixture of sadness and disbelief. We continued with our meal, but his image lingered in my mind. We finished our meal and went our separate ways. I had errands to do and quickly set out to accomplish them.

I glanced toward the town's square, looking somewhat half-heartedly for the strange visitor. I was fearful, knowing that seeing him again would call some response. I drove through town and saw nothing of him. I made some purchases at a store and got back in my car.

Deep within me, the Spirit of God kept speaking to me: "Don't go back to the office until you've at least driven once more around the square."

And so, with some hesitancy, I headed back into town. As I turned the square's third corner, I saw him. He was standing on the steps of the storefront church, going through his sack. I stopped and looked; feeling both compelled to speak to him, yet wanting to drive on.

The empty parking space on the corner seemed to be a sign from God: an invitation to park. I pulled in, got out and approached the town's newest visitor. "Looking for the pastor?" I asked.

"Not really," he replied, "just resting."
"Have you eaten today?"
"Oh, I ate something early this morning."
"Would you like to have lunch with me?"
"Do you have some work I could do for you?"
"No work," I replied. "I commute here to work from the city, but I would like to take you to lunch."
"Sure," he replied with a smile.

As he began to gather his things, I asked some surface questions.
"Where're you heading?"
"St. Louis."
"Where're you from?"
"Oh, all over; mostly Florida."
"How long you've been walking?"
"Fourteen years," came the reply.

I knew I had met someone unusual. We sat across from each other in the same restaurant I had left earlier.

His face was weathered slightly beyond his 38 years. His eyes were dark yet clear, and he spoke with an eloquence and articulation that was startling. He removed his jacket to reveal a bright red T-shirt that said, "Jesus is The Never Ending Story."

Then Daniel's story began to unfold. He had seen rough times early in life. He'd made some wrong choices and reaped the consequences. Fourteen years earlier, while backpacking across the country, he had stopped on the beach in Daytona. He tried to get a job with some men who were putting up a large tent and some equipment. A concert, he thought. He was hired.

The tent did not host a concert, but rather, revival services, where he saw life more clearly. He gave his life over to God. "Nothing's been the same since," he said. "I felt the Lord telling me to keep walking, and so I did, some 14 years now."

"Ever think of stopping?" I asked.

"Oh, once in a while, when it seems to get the best of me. But God has given me this calling. I give out Bibles. That's what's in my sack. I work to buy food and Bibles, and I give them out when His Spirit leads."

I sat amazed. My homeless friend was not homeless. He was on a mission and lived this way by choice. The question burned inside for a moment and then I asked, "What's it like?"
"What?"
"To walk into a town carrying all your things on your back and to show your sign?"
"Oh, it was humiliating at first. People would stare and make comments. Once someone tossed a piece of half-eaten bread and made a gesture that certainly didn't make me feel welcome. But then it became humbling to realize that God was using me to touch lives and change people's concepts of other folks like me."

My concept was changing, too. We finished our dessert and gathered his things. Just outside the door, he paused. He turned to me and said, "Come Ye blessed of my Father and inherit the kingdom I've prepared for you. For when I was hungry you gave me food, when I was thirsty you gave me drink, a stranger and you took me in." I felt as if we were on holy ground.

"Could you use another Bible?" I asked.

He said he preferred a certain translation. It travelled well and was not too heavy. It was also his personal favourite. "I've read through it 14 times," he said.

"I'm not sure we've got one of those, but let's stop by our church and see." I was able to find my new friend a Bible that would do well, and he seemed very grateful. "Where are you headed to from here?"

"Well, I found this little map on the back of this amusement park coupon."
"Are you hoping to work there for awhile?"
"No, I just figure I should go there. I figure someone under those stars, right there, needs a Bible. So that's where I'm going next."

He smiled, and the warmth of his spirit radiated the sincerity of his mission. I drove him back to the town's square where we'd met two hours earlier, and as we drove, it started raining. We parked and unloaded his things.

"Would you sign my autograph book?" he asked. "I like to keep messages from folks I meet."

I wrote in his little book that his commitment to his calling had touched my life. I encouraged him to stay strong. And I left him with a verse of scripture from Jeremiah, "I know the plans I have for you," declared the Lord, "plans to prosper you and not to harm you. Plans to give you a future and a hope."

"Thanks, man," he said. He put his things on his back, smiled his winning smile and said, "See you in the New Jerusalem."

"I'll be there!" was my reply.

He began his journey again. He headed away with his sign dangling from his bedroll and pack of Bibles. He stopped, turned and said, "When you see something that makes you think of me, will you pray for me?"
"You bet," I shouted back, "God bless."
"God bless." And that was the last I saw of him.

Late that evening as I left my office, the wind blew strong. The cold front had settled hard upon the town. I bundled up and hurried to my car. As I sat back and reached for the handbrake, I saw them: a pair of well-worn brown work gloves neatly laid over the length of the handle. I picked them up and thought of my friend and wondered if his hands would stay warm that night without them. I remembered his words: "If you see something that makes you think of me, will you pray for me?"

Today his gloves lie on my desk in my office. They remind me to see the world and its people in a different way, and they help me remember those two hours with my unique friend and to pray for his ministry.

"See you in the New Jerusalem" he said. Yes, Daniel, I know I will!

\*\*\*

*I shall pass this way but once. Therefore, any good that I can do or any kindness that I can show, let me do it now, for I shall not pass this way again. (Stephen Grellet)*

\*\*\*

*Father, I ask you to bless my friends, relatives, e-mail buddies and the one reading this right now. Show them a new revelation of your love and power. Holy Spirit, I ask you to minister to their spirit at this very moment. Where there is pain, give them your peace and mercy. Where there is self-doubt, release a renewed confidence through your grace, in Jesus' precious name.*

Amen.

# WHY GO TO CHURCH?

 A Churchgoer wrote a letter to the editor of a newspaper and complained that it made no sense to go to church every week.

"I've gone for 30 years now," he wrote, "and in that time I have heard something like 3,000 sermons. But for the life of me, I can't remember a single one of them. So, I think I'm wasting my time and the pastors are wasting theirs by giving sermons at all."

This started a real controversy in the "Letters to the Editor" column, much to the delight of the editor. It went on for weeks until someone wrote this clincher:

"I've been married for 30 years now. In that time, my wife has cooked some 32,000 meals. But for the life of me, I cannot recall the entire menu for a single one of those meals. But I do know this: they all nourished me and gave me the strength I needed to do my work. If my wife had not given me these meals, I would be physically dead today. Likewise, if I had not gone to church for nourishment, I would be spiritually dead today!"

When you are down to nothing, God is up to something.

Faith sees the invisible, believes the incredible and receives the impossible.

Thank God for our physical and our spiritual nourishment.

"When Satan is knocking at your door, simply say, "Jesus, could you get that for me?

# CHOOSE ETERNAL LIFE

 After a few of the usual Sunday evening hymns, the church's pastor slowly stood up, walked over to the pulpit and, before he gave his sermon for the evening, briefly introduced a guest minister who was in the service that evening.

In the introduction, the pastor told the congregation that the guest minister was one of his dearest childhood friends and that he wanted him to have a few moments to greet the church and share whatever he felt would be appropriate for the service. With that, an elderly man stepped up to the pulpit and began to speak.

"A father, his son, and a friend of his son were sailing off the Pacific coast," he began, "when a fast approaching storm blocked any attempt to get back to the shore. The waves were so high, that even though the father was an experienced sailor, he could not keep the boat upright and the three were swept into the ocean as the boat capsised."

The old man hesitated for a moment, making eye contact with two teenagers who were, for the first time since the service began, looking somewhat interested in his story. The aging minister continued with his story.

"Grabbing a rescue line, the father had to make the most excruciating decision of his life: to which boy would he throw the other end of the life line.

"He only had seconds to make the decision. The father knew that his son was a Christian and he also knew that his son's friend was not.

"The agony of his decision could not be matched by the torrent of waves. As the father yelled out, 'I love you, son!' he threw out the life-line to his son's friend.

"By the time the father had pulled the friend back to the capsized boat, his son had disappeared beneath the raging swells, into the black of night. His body was never recovered."

By this time, the two teenagers were sitting up straight in the pew, anxiously waiting for the next words to come out of the old minister's mouth.

"The father," he continued, "knew his son would have eternal life with Jesus and he could not bear the thought of his son's friend stepping into an eternity without Jesus.

"Therefore, he sacrificed his son to save the son's friend. How great is the love of God that he should do the same for us. Our heavenly father sacrificed his only begotten son that we could be saved. I urge you to accept his offer to rescue you; take a hold of the life-line He is throwing out to you in this service."

With that, the old man turned and sat back down in his chair as silence filled the room.

The pastor again walked slowly to the pulpit and delivered a brief sermon with an invitation at the end. However, no one responded to the appeal.

Within minutes after the service ended, the two teenagers were at the old man's side.

"That was a nice story," politely stated one of them, "but I don't think it was very realistic for a father to give up his only son's life in the hope that the other boy would become a Christian." "Well, you've got a point there," the old man replied, glancing down at his worn Bible. A big smile broadened his narrow face. He once again looked up at the boys and said, "It sure isn't very realistic, is it? But I'm here today to tell you that story gives me a glimpse of what it must have been like for God to give up His son for me. You see, I was that father and your Pastor is my son's friend."

# NO COINCIDENCE

The brand new pastor and his wife, assigned to their first ministry to reopen a church in suburban Brooklyn, arrived in early October, excited about their opportunities.

When they saw their church, it was very run down and needed much work. They set a goal to have everything done in time to have their first service on Christmas Eve. They worked hard, repairing pews, plastering walls and painting. By December 18, they were ahead of schedule and just about finished.

However, on December 19 a terrible rainstorm hit the area and lasted for two days. So, on the 21st, the pastor went over to the church to see how it had suffered.

His heart sank when he saw that the roof had leaked, causing a large area of plaster about 20 feet by 8 feet to fall off the front wall of the sanctuary just behind the pulpit, beginning  from about head high. The pastor cleaned up the mess on the floor, and not knowing what else to do but postpone the Christmas Eve service, he headed home.

On the way, he noticed that a local business was having a flea market-type sale for charity, so he stopped by. One of the items was a beautiful, handmade, ivory-coloured, crocheted tablecloth with exquisite work, fine colours and a cross embroidered right in the centre. It was just the right size to cover up the hole in the front wall.

He bought it and headed back to the church. By this time it had started to snow. An old woman running from the opposite direction was trying to catch the bus but she just missed it. So the pastor invited her to wait in the warm church for the next bus, 45 minutes later. She sat in a pew and paid no attention to the pastor while he got a ladder, and other bits and pieces to put up the tablecloth as a wall tapestry. The pastor could hardly believe how beautiful it looked and how it covered up the entire problem area. Then he noticed the woman walking down the centre aisle, her face was like a sheet.

"Pastor," she asked, "where did you get that tablecloth?"

The pastor explained. The woman asked him to check the lower right corner to see if the initials, EBG were crocheted there. They were. These were the initials of the woman, and she had made this tablecloth 35 years before in Austria. The woman could hardly believe it as the pastor told how he had just gotten the tablecloth.

The woman explained that before the war she and her husband were well-to-do people in Austria. When the Nazis came, she was forced to leave. Her husband was going to follow her the next week. But she was captured, sent to prison and never saw her husband or her home again. The pastor wanted to give her the tablecloth, but she made the pastor keep it for the church. The pastor insisted on driving her home; that was the least he could do. She lived on the other side of Staten Island and was only in Brooklyn for the day for a housecleaning job.

What a wonderful service they had on Christmas Eve. The church was almost full and the music and the spirit were great. At the end of the service, the pastor and his wife greeted everyone at the door and many said that they would return. One older man, whom the pastor recognised from the neighbourhood, continued to sit in one of the pews and stare, and the pastor wondered why he wasn't leaving.

The man asked him where he got the tablecloth on the front wall, because it was identical to one that his wife had made years ago when they lived in Austria, before the war, and how could there be two tablecloths so much alike? He told the pastor how the Nazis came, how he forced his wife to flee for her safety and he was supposed to follow her, but he was arrested and put in a prison. He never saw his wife or his home again for all the 35 years in between. The pastor asked him if he would allow him to take him for a little ride.

They drove to Staten Island, to the same house where the pastor had taken the woman three days earlier. He helped the man climb the three flights of stairs to the woman's apartment, knocked on the door and he saw the greatest Christmas reunion he could ever imagine.

[True Story - submitted by Pastor Rob Reid]

# I WISH YOU ENOUGH

At an airport, I overheard a father and his daughter in their last moments together. They had announced her plane's departure and standing near the door she said, "Daddy, our lives together has more than enough. Your love is all I ever needed. I wish you enough too, Daddy."

They kissed goodbye and she left. He walked over towards the window where I was seated. Standing there I could see he wanted to cry. I tried not to intrude on his privacy, but he welcomed me in by asking, "Have you ever said goodbye to someone knowing it would be forever?"

"Yes, I have." I replied. Saying that, brought back memories I had of my expressing my love and appreciation for all that my Dad had done for me. Recognising that his days were limited, I took the time to tell him face to face how much he meant to me. So I knew what this man was experiencing.

"Forgive me for asking, but why is this a forever goodbye?" I asked.

"I am old and she lives much too far away. I have challenges ahead and the reality is that her next trip back will be for my funeral," he said.

"When you were saying goodbye, I heard you say, "I wish you enough." May I ask what that means?"

He began to smile. "That's a wish that has been handed down from other generations. My parents used to say it to everyone."

He paused for a moment and looked up, as if trying to remember it in detail. He smiled even more. "When we said, "I wish you enough," we were wanting the other person to have a life filled with enough good things to sustain them."

Turning toward me, he shared the following as if he were reciting it from memory:
"I wish you enough sun to keep your attitude bright.
I wish you enough rain to appreciate the sun more.
I wish you enough happiness to keep your spirit alive.
I wish you enough pain so that the smallest joys in life appear much bigger.
I wish you enough gain to satisfy your wanting.
I wish you enough loss to appreciate all that you possess.
I wish you enough 'hellos' to get you through the final 'goodbye'."

He then began to sob and walked away.

To you, the reader of this book, I wish you enough.

# BLIND, YET I SEE CLEARLY

The 92-year-old, petite, well-poised and proud lady, who was fully dressed each morning by eight o'clock, with her hair fashionably coifed and makeup perfectly applied, even though she was legally blind, moved to a nursing home one day.

Her husband of 70 years had recently passed away, making the move necessary. After many hours of waiting patiently in the lobby of the nursing home, she smiled when told her room was ready.

As she manoeuvred her walker to the elevator, I provided a visual description of her tiny room, including the eyelet sheets that had been hung on her window.

"I love it," she stated with the enthusiasm of an eight-year-old having just been presented with a new puppy. "Mrs. Jones, you haven't seen the room, just wait."

"That doesn't have anything to do with it," she replied. "Happiness is something you decide on ahead of time. Whether I like my room or not doesn't depend on how the furniture is arranged, it's how I arrange my mind. I have already decided to love it. It's a decision I make every morning when I wake up. I have a choice: I can spend the day in bed, recounting the difficulty I have with the parts of my body that no longer work; or get out of bed and be thankful for the ones that do. Each day is a gift, and as long as my eyes open I'll focus on the new day and all the happy memories I've stored away just for this time in my life.

Old age is like a bank account. You withdraw from what you've put in.
"So, my advice to you would be to deposit a lot of happiness in the bank account of memories. Thank you for your part in filling my memory bank. I'm still depositing."

Remember the five simple rules to be happy:

1. Free your heart from hatred.
2. Free your mind from worries.
3. Live simply.
4. Give more.
5. Expect less.

# GOD'S IMAGE IN YOU

*Malachi 3:3: He will sit as a refiner and purifier of silver.*

This verse puzzled some women in a Bible study group, and they wondered what this statement meant about the character and nature of God. One of the women offered to find out the process of refining silver and report back to the group at their next Bible study.

That week, the woman called a silversmith and made an appointment to watch him at work. She didn't mention anything about the reason for her interest beyond her curiosity about the process of refining silver.

As she watched the silversmith, he held a piece of silver over the fire and let it heat up. He explained that in refining silver, one needed to hold the silver in the middle of the fire where the flame is hot.

The woman thought about God holding us in such a hot spot and then she thought again about the verse: "He sits as a refiner and purifier of silver."

She asked the silversmith if it was true that he had to sit there in front of the fire the whole time the silver was being refined.

The man answered, "Yes", and that he not only had to sit there holding the silver, but he had to keep his eyes on the silver the entire time it was in the fire. If the silver was left a moment too long in the flames, it would be destroyed.

The woman was silent for a moment. Then she asked the silversmith, "How do you know when the silver is fully refined?"
He smiled at her and answered, "Oh, that's easy - when I see my image in it."

If today you are feeling the heat of the fire, remember that God has His eye on you and will keep watching until He sees His image in you.

# HONOUR GOD'S NAME

Several years ago, a friend of mine and her husband were invited to spend the weekend at the husband's employer's home. My friend, Arlene, was nervous about the weekend. The boss was very wealthy, with a fine home on the waterway and cars costing more than her house.

The first day and evening went well, and Arlene was delighted to have this rare glimpse into how the very wealthy live. The husband's employer was quite generous as a host, and took them to the finest restaurants. Arlene knew she would never have the opportunity to indulge in this kind of extravagance again, so was enjoying herself immensely.

As the three of them were about to enter an exclusive restaurant that evening, the boss was walking slightly ahead of Arlene and her husband. He stopped suddenly, looking down on the pavement for a long, silent moment.

Arlene wondered if she was supposed to pass him. There was nothing on the ground except a single darkened penny that someone had dropped, and a few cigarette butts. Still silent, the man reached down and picked up the penny. He held it up and smiled, then put it in his pocket as if he had found a great treasure. How absurd! What need did this man have for a penny? Why would he even take the time to stop and pick it up?

Throughout dinner, the entire scene nagged at her. Finally, she could stand it no longer. She causally mentioned that her daughter once had a coin collection, and asked if the penny he had found had been of some value.

A smile crept across the man's face as he reached into his pocket for the penny and held it out for her to see. She had seen many pennies before! What was the point of this?

"Look at it," he said. "Read what it says."

She read the words, "United States of America."

"No, not that. Read further."

"One cent?"

"No, keep reading."

"In God we Trust?"

"Yes!"

"And?"

"And if I trust in God, the name of God is holy, even on a coin. Whenever I find a coin I see that inscription. It is written on every single United States coin, but we never seem to notice it! God drops a message right in front of me telling me to trust Him? Who am I to pass it by? When I see a coin, I pray; I stop to see if my trust is in God at that moment. I pick the coin up as a response to God; that I do trust in Him. For a short time, at least, I cherish it as if it were gold. I think it is God's way of starting a conversation with me.

Lucky for me, God is patient and pennies are plentiful!"

When I was out shopping today, I found a penny on the sidewalk. I stopped and picked it up, and realised that I had been worrying and fretting in my mind about things I cannot change. I read the words, "In God we Trust," and had to laugh. Yes, God, I get the message. It seems that I have been finding an inordinate number of pennies in the last few months, but then again, pennies are plentiful!

And God is patient...

The best mathematical equation I have ever seen:

1 cross  + 3 nails  =  4 given

# THE BIBLE SPEAKS

A boy was sitting on a park bench with one hand resting on an open Bible. He was loudly exclaiming his praise to God. "Hallelujah! Hallelujah! God is great!" he yelled without worrying whether anyone heard him or not.

Shortly after, along came a man who had recently completed some studies at a local university. Feeling very enlightened in the ways of truth and very eager to show this enlightenment, he asked the boy about the source of his joy.

"Hey," asked the boy in return with a bright laugh, "Do you have any idea what God is able to do?

"I just read that God opened up the waves of the Red Sea and led the whole nation of Israel right through the middle!"

The enlightened man laughed lightly, sat down next to the boy and began to try to open his eyes to the "realities" of the miracles of the Bible. "That can all be very easily explained. Modern scholarship has shown that the Red Sea in that area was only 10 inches deep at that time. It was no problem for the Israelites to wade across."

The boy was stumped. His eyes wandered from the man back to the Bible lying open on his lap. The man, content that he had enlightened a poor, naive young person to the finer points of scientific insight turned to leave.

Scarcely had he taken two steps when the boy began to rejoice and praise even louder than before. The man turned to ask the reason for this resumed jubilation.

"Wow!" exclaimed the boy happily, "God is greater than I thought! Not only did He lead the whole nation of Israel through the Red Sea, He topped it off by drowning the whole Egyptian army in 10 inches of water!"

# GOD ALWAYS PROVIDES

On Christmas Eve, I hurried to go to the supermarket to buy the gifts I hadn't managed to buy earlier. When I saw all the people there, I started to complain to myself: "It's going to take forever here and I still have so many other places to go. Christmas really is getting more and more annoying every year. How I wish I could just lie down, go to sleep and only wake up after it."

Nonetheless, I made my way to the toy section, and there started to curse the prices, wondering if kids really play with such expensive toys. While looking in the toy section, I noticed a small boy of about five years old, pressing a doll against his chest. He kept on touching the hair of the doll and looked so sad. I wondered who this doll was for. Then the little boy turned to the old woman next to him: "Granny, are you sure I don't have enough money?" The old lady replied: "You know that you don't have enough money to buy this doll, my dear." Then she asked him to stay there for five minutes while she went to look around. She left quickly. The little boy was still holding the doll in his hand.

Finally, I started to walk towards him and I asked him who he wanted to give this doll to. "It is the doll that my sister loved most and wanted so much for this Christmas. She was so sure that Santa Claus would bring it to her." I replied to him that maybe Santa Claus will bring it to her after all. But he replied to me sadly, "No, Santa Claus can't bring it to her where she is now. I have to give the doll to my mother so that she can give it to her when she goes there." His eyes were so sad while saying this. "My sister has gone to be with God. Daddy says that Mummy will also go to see God very soon, so I thought that she could take the doll with her to give it to my sister." My heart nearly stopped. The little boy looked up at me and said: "I told Daddy to tell Mummy not to go yet. I asked him to wait until I came back from the supermarket." Then he showed me a very nice photo of him where he was laughing. He then told me: "I also want Mummy to take this photo with her so that she won't forget me. I love my mummy and I wish she didn't have to leave me, but Daddy says that she has to go to be with my little sister." He looked again at the doll with sad eyes. I quickly reached for my wallet and took a few notes and said to the boy. "What if we checked again, just in case if you have enough money?"

"Okay," he said. "I hope that I have enough."

I added some of my money to his without him seeing and we started to count it. There was enough for the doll, and even some left over. The little boy said: "Thank you God for giving me enough money."

Then he looked at me and added: "I asked yesterday, before I went to sleep, for God to make sure I have enough money to buy this doll so that Mummy can give it to my sister. He heard me. I also wanted to have enough money to buy a white rose for my Mummy, but didn't dare to ask God too much. But He gave me enough to buy the doll and

74

the white rose. You know, my Mummy loves white roses."

A few minutes later, the old lady came back again and I left with my trolley. I finished my shopping in a totally different state from when started. I couldn't get the little boy out of my mind. Then I remembered a local newspaper article two days ago, which mentioned a drunken man in a truck, who hit a car carrying a young lady and a little girl. The little girl died right away, and the mother was left in a critical state. The family had to decide whether to pull the plug on the life-assisting machine, because the young lady would not be able to get out of the coma. Was this the family of the little boy?

Two days after this encounter with the little boy, I read that the young lady had passed away. I couldn't stop myself and went to buy a bunch of white roses and I went to the mortuary where the body of the young woman could be viewed before burial. She was there, in her coffin, holding a beautiful white rose in her hand with the photo of the little boy and the doll placed over her chest. I left the place crying, feeling that my life had been changed forever.

The love that this little boy had for his mother and his sister is still, to this day, hard to imagine. But God's love is greater. He allowed Jesus to die on the cross, so that we might live.

# THE PRICE OF A GIFT

A wealthy man and his son loved to collect rare works of art. They had everything in their collection, from Picasso to Raphael. They would often sit together and admire the great works of art.

When the Vietnam conflict broke out, the son went to war. He was very courageous and died in battle while rescuing another soldier. The father was notified and grieved deeply for his only son.

About a month later, just before Christmas, there was a knock at the door. A young man stood at the door with a large package in his hands. He said, "Sir, you don't know me, but I am the soldier for whom your son gave his life. He saved many lives that day, and he was carrying me to safety when a bullet struck him in the heart and he died instantly. He often talked about you and your love for art." The young man held out a package. "I know this isn't much. I'm not really a great artist, but I think your son would have wanted you to have this."

The father opened the package. It was a portrait of his son, painted by the young man. He stared in awe at the way the soldier had captured the personality of his son in the painting. The father was so drawn to the eyes that his own eyes welled up with tears. He thanked the young man and offered to pay him for the picture. "Oh, no sir, I could never repay what your son did for me. It's a gift."

The father hung the portrait over his mantle piece. Every time visitors came to his home he took them to see the portrait of his son before he showed them any of the other great works he had collected.

The man died a few months later. There was to be a great auction of his paintings. Many influential people gathered, excited over seeing the great paintings and having an opportunity to purchase one for their collection.

On the platform sat the painting of the son. The auctioneer pounded his gavel. "We will start the bidding with this picture of the son. Who will bid for this picture?"

There was silence. Then a voice in the back of the room shouted, "We want to see the famous paintings. Skip this one."

But the auctioneer persisted. "Will somebody bid for this painting? Who will start the bidding? $100, $200?"

Another voice angrily shouted, "We didn't come to see this painting. We came to see the Van Goghs, the Rembrandts. Get on with the real bids!"

But still the auctioneer continued. "The son! The son! Who'll take the son?"

Finally, a voice came from the very back of the room. It was the long-time gardener of the man and his son. "I'll give $10 for the painting." Being a poor man, it was all he could afford.

"We have 10, who will bid $20?"
"Give it to him for $10. Let's see the masters."
"$10 is the bid, won't someone bid $20?"
The crowd was becoming angry. They didn't want the picture of the son. They wanted the more worthy investments for their collections.

The auctioneer pounded the gavel. "Going once, twice, SOLD for $10!"

A man sitting on the second row shouted, "Now let's get on with the collection!"

The auctioneer laid down his gavel. "I'm sorry, the auction is over."
"What about the paintings?"
"I am sorry. When I was called to conduct this auction, I was told of a secret stipulation in the will. I was not allowed to reveal that stipulation until this time. Only the painting of the son would be auctioned. Whoever bought that painting would inherit the entire estate, including the paintings. The man who took the son gets everything!"

\*\*\*

God gave His son 2,000 years ago to die on the cross. Much like the auctioneer, His message today is: "The Son, the Son, who'll take the Son?" Because, you see, whoever takes the Son gets everything.

*For God so Loved the world He gave His only begotten Son, whosoever believeth, shall have eternal life (John 3: 16).*

That's Love!

# PEDAL IN TANDEM WITH CHRIST

At first, I saw God as my observer, my judge, keeping track of the things I did wrong, so as to know whether I merited heaven or hell when I die.

He was out there sort of like a president; I recognised His picture when I saw it, but I really didn't know Him. But later on, when I met Christ, it seemed as though life were rather like a bike ride, but it was a tandem bike, and I noticed that Christ was in the back helping me to pedal. I don't know just when it was that He suggested we change places, but life has not been the same since.

When I had control, I knew the way. It was rather boring, but predictable. It was the shortest distance between two points. But when He took the lead, He knew delightful long cuts, up mountains, and through rocky places at breakneck speeds. All I could do was hang on!

Even though it looked like madness He said, "Pedal!" I worried and was anxious and asked, "Where are you taking me?" He laughed and didn't answer, and I started to learn to trust. I forgot my boring life and entered into the adventure, and when I'd say, "I'm scared," He'd lean back and touch my hand. I gained love, peace, acceptance and joy; gifts to take on my journey, My Lord's and mine. And we were off again.

He said, "Give the gifts away. They're extra baggage, too much weight." So I did, to the people we met, and I found that in giving I received, and still our burden was light.

I did not trust Him at first to take control of my life. I thought He'd wreck it; but he knows bike secrets, knows how to make it bend to take sharp corners, knows how to jump to clear high rocks, knows how to fly to shorten scary passages. And I am learning to shut up and pedal in the strangest places. I'm beginning to enjoy the view and the cool breeze on my face with my delightful constant companion, Jesus Christ.

And when I'm sure I just can't do it anymore, He just smiles and says, "Pedal."

# MARIJA ILIJOSKA'S TESTIMONY

I would like to share an experience I had with God and I hope that this will stay with you and that one day it may help you in a difficult situation.

One morning I had to get up very early to go to work.  My friends used to come and pick me up from Newbold College, but that morning my alarm didn't ring because I hadn't set it correctly.  My friends waited for me but, of course, after a while they had to leave.

When I woke up I realised I was an hour late so I started to pray that I would find somebody who was going to Bracknell bus station.  I had just started to walk when I saw one of my friends who was going to Bracknell and they kindly gave me a lift.

However, when I arrived at the bus station, I realised I'd left my wallet behind and so I didn't have any money with me.  What did I do?  I started praying again!  As far as I was concerned, the only solution was to walk back to Newbold to get my wallet, but I still kept praying for help.  Then I saw a student from Newbold, so I decided to ask her to let me use her mobile, because mine wasn't working properly. But before I could talk to her, her bus came and she left! I continued to pray but was more specific this time. I asked for 20p so that I could phone a friend to come and get me from the bus station. I had only taken about two steps when I saw a one pound coin on the ground. I picked it up and went straight to the phone box without even saying thank you to the Lord.

I put in my money, dialled my friend's number and got the answering machine, which means I'd lost that pound.

I started talking to the Lord again, telling him how big a sinner I was and how bad I was for not even saying thank you. At that moment I decided to ask for help again, even though my hope was at rock bottom.

I began walking back to Newbold. As I was passing Bentalls, I heard my name called. When I look towards the sound, I saw the friend who had given me the lift into Bracknell working in the window. I asked him if he could lend me some money and his boss kindly came out and gave me the money for my bus fare.

I told his boss everything that had happened to me that morning and mentioned the Lord. He listened to me very carefully and told me I was very lucky. But I feel my God is my source of 'luck' – if you can call it that.
At that moment I realised that when I'd first arrived at the bus station I'd had only 10 or 15

minutes before the next bus. However, things had happened so fast that I still had time to catch the bus. So I ran back to the bus station and got on the bus with one minute to spare.

I gave the money to the driver, but he didn't have any change to give me. He told me to take a seat and so, after all that, I didn't even have to pay the bus fare!

That day was an important day for me. It was yet another experience that made me very happy: it taught me and proved to me that no matter what is happening, I need to keep on praying, even if I have made a mistake.

May God bless all of you as he blessed me on that day and strengthened my faith.

October 2003
Newbold Church Service
Binfield, Berkshire

# PRAISE GOD FOR CLOSED DOORS

We need to learn to thank the Lord for closed doors as we do an open door.

The reason God closes doors is because He has not prepared anything over there for us. If he didn't close the wrong door we would never find our way to the right door. Even when we don't realise it, God directs our paths through the closing and opening of doors.

When one door closes, it forces us to change our course. Another door closes; it forces us to change our course yet again. Then finally, we find the open door and walk right into our blessing. But instead of praising God for the closed door (which kept us out of trouble), we get upset because we "judge by the appearances." And in our own arrogance, or ignorance, we insist that we know what is right.

We have a very present help in the time of need, who is always standing guard. Because He walks ahead of us, He can see trouble down the road and He sets up roadblocks (closed doors) and detours accordingly.

But through our lack of wisdom, we try to tear down the roadblocks or push aside the detour signs. Then the minute we get into trouble, we start crying, "Lord how could this happen to me?" We have got to realise that the closed door was a blessing. Didn't He say, "No good thing will He withhold from them that love him?"

If you get sacked from your job, don't be downhearted. Instead thank God for the new opportunities that will manifest themselves - it might be a better job, or an opportunity to go to school.

If that man or woman won't return your call - it might not be them, it might be the Lord setting up a roadblock (just let it go).

One time a person had a bank he had been doing business with for many years tell him, "No," for a £10,000 loan. The Lord led him to call another bank. That bank approved a £40,000 loan for him at a lower interest rate than his own bank had advertised.

I'm so grateful, for the many times God has closed doors on me, just to open them in the most unexpected places.

*Remember*:

God gives you . . .
. Enough happiness to keep you sweet
· Enough trials to keep you strong
· Enough sorrows to keep you human
· Enough hope to keep you happy

- Enough failure to keep you humble
- Enough success to keep you eager
- Enough friends to give you comfort
- Enough wealth to meet your needs
- Enough enthusiasm to make you look forward
- Enough faith to banish depression, and
- Enough determination to make each day a better day than the last.

*The Lord orders the steps of a good person, and He delights in his/her way. (Psalm 37:23)*

# PAID IN FULL

A young man was getting ready to graduate from college.

For many months, he had admired a beautiful sports car in a dealer's showroom, and knowing his father could well afford it, he told him that was all he wanted.

As Graduation Day approached, the young man awaited signs that his father had purchased the car.

Finally, on the morning of his graduation his father called him into his private study. His father told him how proud he was to have such a fine son, and told him how much he loved him. He handed his son a beautifully wrapped gift box. Curious, but somewhat disappointed the young man opened the box and found a lovely, leather-bound Bible.

Angrily, he raised his voice at his father and said, "With all your money, you give me a Bible?" and stormed out of the house, leaving the holy book.

Many years passed and the young man was very successful in business. He had a beautiful home and wonderful family, but realised his father was very old, and thought perhaps he should go to him.

He had not seen him since that graduation day. But before he could make arrangements, he received a telegram telling him his father had passed away, and willed all of his possessions to his son. He needed to come home immediately and take care of things.

When he arrived at his father's house, sudden sadness and regret filled his heart. He began to search his father's important papers and saw the still new Bible, just as he had left it years ago. With tears, he opened the Bible, and began to turn the pages when a car key dropped from an envelope taped behind the Bible. It had a tag with the dealer's name, the same dealer who had the sports car he had desired. On the tag was the date of his graduation, and the words ... PAID IN FULL.

*** 

How many times do we miss God's blessings because they are not packaged as we expected?

# EACH DAY IS SPECIAL

A friend of mine opened his wife's underwear
drawer and picked up a silk paper wrapped
package:

"This," he said, "isn't any ordinary package."

He unwrapped the box and stared at both the
silk paper and the box.

"She got this the first time we went to New York,
eight or nine years ago. She never put it on. Was
saving it for a special occasion. Well, I guess this
is it. He got near the bed and placed the gift box
next to the other clothing he was taking to the
funeral house. His wife had just died. He turned
to me and said:

"Never save something for a special occasion.
Every day in your life is a special occasion".

I think those words changed my life.
Now I read more and clean less. I sit on the
porch without worrying about anything.
I spend more time with my family, and less at
work.

I understand that life should be a source of
experience to be lived up to, not survived
through. I use crystal glasses every day. I'll wear

new clothes to go to the supermarket, if I feel like it.

I don't save my special perfume for special occasions; I use it whenever I want to. The words "Someday..." and "One Day..." are fading away from my dictionary. If it's worth seeing, listening or doing, I want to see, listen or do it now.

I don't know what my friend's wife would have done if she knew she wouldn't be there the next morning; this nobody can tell. I think she might have called her relatives and closest friends.

She might call old friends to make peace over past quarrels. I'd like to think she would go out for her favourite food. It's these small things that I would regret not doing, if I knew my time had come.

I would regret it, because I would no longer see the friends I would meet letters... letters that I wanted to write "one of these days". I would regret and feel sad, because I didn't say to my family, how much I love them.

Now, I try not to delay, postpone or keep anything that could bring laughter and joy into our lives. And every morning, when I open my eyes, I tell myself that it is special.

Every day, every minute, every breath truly is a gift from God.

# SPEAK UP FOR JESUS

There was once a professor of philosophy, who was a deeply committed atheist.

His primary goal for one required class was to spend the entire semester attempting to prove that God didn't exist. His students were always afraid to argue with him because of his impeccable logic.

For twenty years, he had taught this class and no one had ever had the courage to go against him. Sure, some had argued in class at times, but no one had ever really gone against him because of his reputation.

At the end of every semester on the last day, he would say to his class of 300 students, "If there is anyone here who still believes in Jesus, stand up!" In twenty years, no one had ever stood up.

They knew what he was going to do next. He would say, "Anyone who believes in God is a fool, because: "If God existed, he could stop this piece of chalk from hitting the ground and breaking. Such a simple task to prove that He is God, and yet He can't do it."

Every year, he would drop the chalk onto the tile floor of the classroom and it would shatter into pieces. All of the students would do nothing but stop and stare.

Most of the students thought that God couldn't exist. Certainly, a number of Christians had slipped through, but for 20 years, they had been too afraid to stand up.

Well, a few years ago there was a freshman who happened to enrol. He was a Christian, and had heard the stories about his professor. He was required to take the class for his major, and he was afraid. But for three months of that semester, he prayed every morning that he would have the courage to stand up no matter what the professor said, or what the class thought. Nothing they said could ever shatter his faith...he hoped.

Finally, the day came. The professor said, "If there is anyone here who still believes in God, stand up!" The professor and the other 299 students looked at the young Christian, shocked, as he stood up at the back of the classroom.

The professor shouted, "You fool! If God existed, he would keep this piece of chalk from breaking when it hit the ground!"

He proceeded to drop the chalk, but as he did, it slipped out of his fingers, off his shirt cuff, onto the pleat of his trousers, down his leg, and off his shoe. As it hit the ground, it simply rolled away unbroken. The professor's jaw dropped as he stared at the chalk. He looked up at the young man, and then ran out of the lecture hall.

The young man who had stood, proceeded to walk to the front of the room and shared his faith in Jesus for the next half hour. 299 students stayed and listened as he told of God's love for them and of His power through Jesus.

# THE ATHEIST'S HOLIDAY

In Florida, an atheist became incensed over the preparation for Easter and Passover holidays, and decided to contact his local ACLU (American Civil Liberties Union) about the discrimination inflicted on atheists by the constant celebrations afforded to Christians and Jews with all their holidays, while the atheists had no holiday to celebrate.

The ACLU jumped on the opportunity to once again pick up the cause of the godless and assigned their sharpest attorneys to the case. The case was brought before a wise judge who after listening to the long, passionate presentation of the ACLU lawyers, promptly banged his gavel and declared, "Case dismissed!"

The lead ACLU lawyer immediately stood and objected to the ruling and said, "Your honour, how can you possibly dismiss this case? Surely the Christians have Christmas, Easter and many other observances. And the Jews - why in addition to Passover they have Yom Kippur and Hanukkah, and yet my client and all other atheists have no such holiday!"

The judge leaned forward in his chair and simply said, "Obviously your client is too confused to know about, or for that matter, even celebrate the atheists' holiday!"

The ACLU lawyer pompously said, "We are aware of no such holiday for atheists. Just when might that be, your honour?"

The judge said, "Well it comes every year on exactly the same date - April 1."

\*\*\*

*The fool says in his heart, 'There is no God.'*
*(Psalm14:1, Psalm 53:1)*

# EVOLUTION EXPLAINED

One day a six-year-old girl was sitting in a classroom. Her teacher was going to explain evolution to the children. The teacher asked a little boy:

TEACHER: Tommy, do you see the tree outside?
TOMMY: Yes.
TEACHER: Do you see the grass outside?
TOMMY: Yes.
TEACHER: Go outside and look up and see if you can see the sky.
TOMMY: Okay. (He returned a few minutes later) Yes, I saw the sky.
TEACHER: Did you see God?
TOMMY: No.
TEACHER: That's my point. We can't see God because he isn't there. He doesn't exist.

A little girl spoke up and wanted to ask the boy some questions. The teacher agreed and the little girl asked the boy:

LITTLE GIRL: Tommy, do you see the tree outside?
TOMMY: Yes.
LITTLE GIRL: Do you see the grass outside?
TOMMY: Yesss (getting tired of the questions by this time).
LITTLE GIRL: Did you see the sky?
TOMMY: Yesss
LITTLE GIRL: Do you see the teacher?
TOMMY: Yes

LITTLE GIRL: Do you see her brain?
TOMMY: No
LITTLE GIRL: Then according to what we were taught today, she must not have one!

*FOR WE WALK BY FAITH, NOT BY SIGHT*

# DOES GOD EXIST?

A man went to a barbershop to have his hair and beard cut as usual. He began to have a good conversation with the barber who attended to him. They talked about so many things and various subjects.

Suddenly, when they touched on the subject of God, the barber said: "Look man, I don't believe that God exists."

"Why do you say that?" asked the customer. "Well, it's so easy, you just have to go out in the street to realise that God does not exist. Tell me, if God exists, would there be so many sick people? Would there be abandoned children? If God exists, there would be no suffering or pain. I can't think of loving a God who permits all of these things."

The customer thought for a moment, but he didn't respond because he did not want to start an argument. The barber finished his job and the customer left the shop. Just after he left the barbershop, he saw a man in the street with long hair and a beard. It was very long, and a long time since he had had his haircut.

He looked dirty and unkempt. The customer entered the barber shop again and he said to the barber, "You know what? Barbers do not exist."

"How can you say they don't exist?" asked the surprised barber. " I am here and I am a barber. Why I just worked on you!"

"No!" the customer exclaimed. "Barbers don't exist, because if they did there would be no people with long hair and beard like that man who is outside."

"Ah, barbers do exist, what happens is that people do not come to me."

"Exactly!"- affirmed the customer. "That's the point! God does exist. What happens is people don't go to Him and do not respond to Him. That's why there's so much pain and suffering in the world."

*You will find me when you seek and search for me with all your heart. ( Deuteronomy 4:29)*

# ORGANIC EVOLUTION EXPOSED

God was sitting in heaven when a scientist said to Him, "God, we don't need you anymore. Science has finally figured out a way to create life out of nothing. In other words, we can now do what you did in the beginning."

"Oh, is that so? Tell me more." replied God.

"Well," said the scientist, "we can take soil and form it into the likeness of you and breath life into it, thus creating man. We can actually make a man."

Well, that's very interesting. Show me how."

So the scientist bent down to the earth and started to mould the soil into the shape of a man.

"No, no, no," interrupted God, "get your own soil."

# NOT I BUT CHRIST

A young man, who had been raised as an atheist, was training to be an Olympic diver. The only religious influence in his life came from his outspoken Christian friend. The young diver never really paid much attention to his friend's sermons, but he heard them often.

One night the diver went to the indoor pool at the college he attended. The lights were all off, but as the pool had big skylights and the moon was bright, there was plenty of light to practice by.

The young man climbed up to the highest diving board, and as he turned his back to the pool on the edge of the board and extended his arms, he saw his shadow on the wall. The shadow of his body was in the shape of a cross. Instead of diving, he knelt down and finally asked God to come into his life. As the young man stood, a maintenance man walked in and turned on the lights.

The pool had been drained for repairs.

*** 

*Lean not onto your own understanding.  The angel of the Lord surrounds them that fears Him and delivers them (Proverbs 3:5)*

# HOW POOR ARE YOU?

One day, a father of a very wealthy family took his son on a trip to the country, with the firm purpose of showing his son how poor people can be. They spent a couple of days and nights on the farm of what would be considered a very poor family.

On their return from their trip, the father asked his son, "How was the trip?"
"It was great, Dad."
"Did you see how poor people can be?" the father asked.
"Oh yeah," said the son.
"So what did you learn from the trip?" asked the father.

The son answered, "I saw that we have one dog and they had four. We have a pool that reaches to the middle of our garden and they have a lake that has no end. We have imported lanterns in our garden and they have the stars at night. Our patio reaches to the front yard and they have the whole horizon.

"We have a small piece of land to live on and they have fields that go beyond our sight. We have servants who serve us, but they serve others.

We buy our food, but they grow theirs. We have walls around our property to protect us, they have friends to protect them."

With this the boy's father was speechless. Then his son added, "Thanks, Dad, for showing me how poor we are."

Too many times we forget what we have and concentrate on what we don't have. What is one person's worthless object is another's prized possession. It is all based on one's perspective. It makes you wonder what would happen if we all give thanks for the bounty we have, instead of worrying about wanting more.

# SLEEPING WITH THE ENEMY

I went out last night. As far as I can remember it was a good night. We danced all night. I've not drank that much for a long time - you know how it is you go out and drink and chill and do whatever. Well, as I think about it, some of you don't know how it is. Some of you don't go out, you're good church folk after all.

Anyway, I woke up this morning and found somebody strange in my bed. If I'm honest that's not as strange as it may sound. But this person troubled me; I'm sure I've met them before. Maybe it was their scent, the feel of their skin or the tone of their voice, something just seemed so familiar to me. Maybe the reason I can't remember is that I'm still a little hung over. I'm telling you, last night was a good night. Well, it would have to be if I managed to bring somebody home with me.

I sat for a long time this morning, just looking, staring at the person lying next to me, trying to figure out why I felt like I knew them, and then I made the connection. I suddenly remembered that I did know them; I'd seen them before. It was a few months ago, but I'd definitely shared my bed with them before.

Ever so often they keep on coming back to me. I just couldn't remember them for two reasons:

they hadn't been by for a while, and so many people come in and out of my house, of my bed, that I lose track.

Just like with this person, when people come to visit me, one of the last things that I hear is that "It won't happen again". They tell me all about their reputation and how they want to turn over a new leaf, get a new start. It's the same story, just from people with different faces. Deep down they're all the same. Usually I just laugh, because only I seem to know how addictive I can be.

I've been doing this for years. I've seen so many different people come and go. Some stay, some leave and never come back. I have my regulars, those that are faithful to me, if that's what you could call it. All I know is that I must be doing something right. Providing good customer service, I guess, because people just keep on coming back for more.

You know, I was telling you about who was in my bed this morning, and I'm sure when I tell you, you won't believe me. But would I lie to you?

Some people don't like me. They seem to think that it's my fault that society is the way that it is: the increase in crime, violence in the home, drugs and of course the sex. Apparently, it's all down to people like me. Personally, I blame the family.

People no longer have any family values. Their children have no respect and then, as parents, they have even less. Things just aren't what they used to be, but why am I complaining? I'm the richest I've been for a long time. If people sorted out their families and paid a little more attention to each other then, maybe I wouldn't have such regular visitors. I see some interesting people come and go. If the walls in this room could talk, they'd tell some interesting stories. Some people are rich, some are poor, some are black, some are white, some are male, others female. I really don't discriminate, but they all have one thing in common: they all want a fix and that fix is me.

I'm sorry I digress. I was supposed to be telling you about the person in my bed this morning. I don't know why it's troubling me this much, but it just is. I've always been this way. I love to talk. Once you get me talking some say that you can't get me to stop. People used to say that they were sure I talked Eve into eating the fruit from the tree. You see, I've done it again. I was supposed to be telling you about the person in my bed.

It was you. Yes, you heard me. The person in my bed last night was you - you with your darling sins and addictions: the little ones, the big ones, all of them. You keep coming back to me. It's always the same. You claim that you're going to give up, but, before long, you're back. You come to satisfy your habit in my bed.

It's funny. It's almost as if you don't seem to realise that each time you climb back into my bed with your old ways and I accept you, a little bit more of you belongs to me.

You just keep on doing it, sleeping with me. Sleeping with the enemy.

Oh, I'm sorry. I forgot to introduce myself: my name is Ms Devil, spelt D-E-V-I-L.

*Lady Flemmings 2003*

# BAD COMPANY CORRUPTS GOOD HABITS

Bad relationships and friendships have destroyed the potential and ability of millions of people. Whoever cannot increase you will eventually decrease you. If they are not taking you higher, then they are dragging you lower. Examine the people occupying time in your life and start separating yourself from the spiritual leeches.

Jesus allowed only two kinds of people in His life: those who ministered to Him and those who received His ministry. Have you noticed that He did not spend time with the Pharisees? They did not minister to Him or listen to Him because they were too religious.

Do you feel worn-out, spiritually dead, and lonely? Who is around you? Is someone sucking the life out of you like a vampire or a tick? Are you walking with someone with whom you cannot even talk? If you cannot share your deepest inner feelings, dreams, and fears with him/her in safety, then there is a problem. You are locked up and dying on the inside, and this kind of friend will not even know it. S/he will just keep on grinning.

Jesus did not hang around that kind of person. You will not receive any life-giving ministry as long as you have a bunch of "zeros" around you. They cannot help you, but they can usually manage to keep anyone else from helping you! They cannot take you anywhere, but with all their bad baggage cluttering your life, they will keep anyone else from even trying to take you to a new place.

You need to move those zeros out of the way! Stop wasting your time with non-productive relationships, and do not feel guilty about making changes. All of them have the same opportunity you had - they can choose Christ and pursue His purposes with all their hearts or they can keep their "zero growth, zero effort, zero results" game plan. The problem is theirs, not yours. You chose Christ and that means you must follow Him with everything you have.

Heavenly Father, thank You for sending Your Son to rescue me from darkness and translate me into the kingdom. Now it is time to report to "basic training." Guide me and strengthen me as I trim away the unproductive or openly evil relationships in my life. Help me to be a powerful witness for You and the kingdom throughout this change of environment. In Jesus' name I pray, amen.

[From the book *Called To Conquer* by Bishop Eddie Long]

# SHMILY

My grandparents were married for over half a century, and played their own special game from the time they had met each other. The goal of their game was to write the word *shmily* in a surprise place for the other to find. They took turns leaving *shmily* around the house, and as soon as one of them discovered it, it was their turn to hide it once more.

They dragged *shmily* with their fingers through the sugar and flour containers to await whoever was preparing the next meal. They smeared it in the dew on the windows overlooking the patio, where my grandma always fed us warm, homemade pudding with blue food colouring.

*Shmily* was written in the steam left on the mirror after a hot shower, where it would reappear bath after bath. Once, my grandmother even unrolled an entire roll of toilet paper to write *shmily* on the very last sheet.

There was no end to the places *shmily* would pop up. Little notes with *shmily* scribbled hurriedly were found on dashboards and car seats, or taped to steering wheels. The notes were stuffed inside shoes and left under pillows. *Shmily* was written in the dust upon the mantel and traced in the ashes of the fireplace. This mysterious word was as much a part of my grandparents' house as the furniture. It took me a long time before I was able to fully appreciate my grandparents' game.

Scepticism has kept me from believing in true love - one that is pure and enduring. However, I never doubted my grandparents' relationship. They had love down to a pat. It was more than their flirtatious little games; it was a way of life. Their relationship was based on a devotion and passionate affection, which not everyone is lucky to experience.

Grandma and grandpa held hands every chance they could. They stole kisses as they bumped into each other in their tiny kitchen. They finished each other's sentences and shared the daily crossword puzzle and word jumble. My grandma whispered to me about how cute my grandpa was, how handsome and old he had grown to be. She claimed that she really knew "how to pick 'em."

Before every meal they bowed their heads and gave thanks, marvelling at their blessings: a wonderful family, good fortune, and each other.

But there was a dark cloud in my grandparents' life: my grandmother had breast cancer. The disease had first appeared ten years earlier. As always, Grandpa was with her every step of the way. He comforted her in their yellow room, painted that way so that she could always be surrounded by sunshine, even when she was too sick to go outside. Now the cancer was again attacking her body. With the help of a cane and my grandfather's steady hand, they went to church every week. But my grandmother grew steadily weaker until finally, she could not leave the house anymore. For a while, grandpa would go to church alone, praying to God to watch over his wife.

Then one day, what we all dreaded finally happened. Grandma was gone.

*Shmily.* It was scrawled in yellow on the pink ribbons of my grandmother's funeral bouquet. As the crowd thinned and the last mourners turned to leave, my aunts, uncles, cousins and other family members came forward and gathered around grandma one last time.

Grandpa stepped up to my grandmother's casket and, taking a shaky breath, he began to sing to her. Through his tears and grief, the song came, a deep and throaty lullaby. Shaking with my own sorrow, I will never forget that moment. For I knew that, although I couldn't begin to fathom the depth of their love, I had been privileged to witness its unmatched beauty.

S-h-m-i-l-y: See How Much I Love You.

# WHY GOD CREATED CHILDREN

To those of us who have children in our lives, whether they are your own, grandchildren, nieces, nephews, or students, here is something to make you chuckle.

Whenever your children are out of control, you can take comfort from the thought that even God's omnipotence did not extend to His own children.

After creating heaven and earth, God created Adam and Eve. And the first thing he said was "DON'T!"

"Don't what?" Adam replied.
"Don't eat the forbidden fruit." God said.
"Forbidden fruit? We, forbidden fruit? Hey Eve! We have forbidden fruit!"
"No way!"
"Yes way!"
"Do NOT eat the fruit!" said God.
"Why?"

"Because it will kill you!" God replied, wondering why He hadn't stopped creation after making the elephants. A few minutes later, God saw His children having an apple break and He was ticked!

"Didn't I tell you not to eat the fruit?" God asked.
"Uh huh," Adam replied.
"Then why did you?" said the Father.
"I don't know," said Eve.
"She started it!" Adam said
"Did not!"
"Did too!"
"DID NOT!"

Having had enough with the two of them, God's punishment was that Adam and Eve should have children of their own. Thus the pattern was set and it has never changed.

But there is reassurance in the story!

If you have persistently and lovingly tried to give children wisdom and they haven't taken it, don't be hard on yourself. If God had trouble raising children, what makes you think it would be a piece of cake for you?

# THINK BEFORE YOU SHOUT

A man came home from work late, tired and irritated, to find his five-year old son waiting for him at the door.

"Daddy, can I ask you a question?"
"Yeah, sure. What is it?" replied the man.
"How much do you make an hour?"
"That's none of your business. Why do you ask such a thing?" the man said angrily.
"I just want to know. Please tell me, how much do you make an hour?" pleaded the little boy.
"If you must know, I make £15 an hour."
"Oh," the little boy replied, with his head down. Looking up, he said, "Daddy, can I please borrow £7.50?"

The father was really annoyed. He shouted, "If the only reason you asked that is so you can borrow some money to buy a silly toy or some other nonsense, then you march yourself straight to your room and go to bed. Think about why you are being so selfish. I work hard everyday for such childish behaviour."

The little boy quietly went to his room and shut the door. The man sat down and started to get even angrier about the little boy's questions. How dare he ask such questions only to get some money? After about an hour or so, the man had calmed down, and started to think:

Maybe there was something he really needed to buy with that £7.50, and he really didn't ask for money very often. The man went to his son's room and quietly opened the door.

"Are you asleep, son?" He asked.
"No Daddy, I'm awake," replied the boy.
"I've been thinking, maybe I was too hard on you earlier," said the man, "It's been a long day and I took out my frustration on you. Here's the £7.50 you asked for."

The little boy sat straight up, smiling. "Oh, thank you Daddy!" He shouted.

Then, reaching under his pillow he pulled out an envelope with some coins. The man, seeing that the boy already had money, started to get angry again. The little boy slowly counted out his money, then looked up at his father.

"Why do you want more money if you already have some?" the father grumbled.
"Because I didn't have enough, but now I do," the little boy replied. "Daddy, I have £15 now. Can I buy an hour of your time? Please come home early tomorrow. I would love to have dinner with you."

***

We should not let time slip through our fingers without having spent some time with those who really matter to us - those close to our hearts. If we die tomorrow, the company that we are working for could easily replace us in a matter of days, if not hours. But the family and friends we left behind will feel the loss for the rest of their lives.

Invest wisely. Invest time in your family.

# THE WOODEN BOWL – STILL A LOT TO LEARN

A frail old man went to live with his son, daughter-in-law, and four-year-old grandson. The old man's hands trembled, his eyesight was blurred and his step faltered.

The family ate together at the table. But the elderly grandfather's shaky hands and failing sight made eating difficult. Peas rolled off his spoon onto the floor. When he held the glass, milk spilled on the tablecloth.

The son and daughter-in-law became irritated with the mess.
"We must do something about grandfather," said the son. "I've had enough of his spilled milk, noisy eating and food on the floor."

So the husband and wife set a small table in the corner. There, grandfather ate alone while the rest of the family enjoyed dinner. Since grandfather had broken a dish or two, his food was served in a wooden bowl. When the family glanced in grandfather's direction, sometimes he had a tear in his eye as he sat alone. Still, the only words the couple had for him were sharp admonitions when he dropped a fork or spilled food.

The four-year-old watched it all in silence. One evening before supper, the father noticed his son playing with wood scraps on the floor. He asked the child sweetly, "What are you making?"

Just as sweetly, the boy responded, "Oh, I am making a little bowl for you and mama to eat your food in when I grow up." The four-year-old smiled and went back to work. The words so struck the parents that they were speechless. Though no word was spoken, both knew what must be done.

That evening the husband took grandfather's hand and gently led him back to the family table. For the remainder of his days he ate every meal with the family. And for some reason, neither husband nor wife seemed to care any longer when a fork was dropped, milk spilled, or the tablecloth was soiled.

# LESSONS

I've learned that, no matter what happens or how bad it seems today, life does go on, and it will be better tomorrow.

I've learned that, regardless of your relationship with your parents, you'll miss them when they're gone from your life.

I've learned that making a 'living' is not the same thing as making a 'life.'

I've learned that life sometimes gives you a second chance.

I've learned that you shouldn't go through life with a catcher's mitten on both hands. You need to be able to throw something back.

I've learned that if you pursue happiness, it will elude you. But, if you focus on your family, your friends, the needs of others, your work and doing the very best you can, happiness will find you.

I've learned that whenever I decide something with an open heart, I usually make the right decision.

I've learned that even when I have pains, I don't have to be one.

I've learned that you shouldn't go through life with a catcher's mitt on both hands; you need to be able to throw some things back.

I've learned that every day, you should reach out and touch someone. People love that human touch - holding hands, a warm hug, or just a friendly pat on the back.

I've learned that I still have a lot to learn.

# JUST ONE LAST RING

Every Sabbath afternoon after the morning service at their church, the pastor and his eleven-year-old son would go out into their town and hand out gospel tracts.

This particular Sabbath afternoon, when it was time for the pastor and his son to go to the streets with their tracts, but it was very cold outside as well as pouring down with rain. The boy bundled up in his warmest clothes and said, "Okay dad, I'm ready."

His dad asked, "Ready for what?"
"Dad, it's time we get our tracts and go out."
"Son, it's very cold outside and it's pouring down rain."
The boy gave his dad a surprised look, asking, "But Dad, aren't people still going to Hell, even though it's raining?"
"Son, I am not going out in this weather."
Despondently, the boy asked, "Dad, can I go? Please?"

His father hesitated for a moment then said, "Okay, you can go. Here are the tracts, and be careful son."
"Thanks Dad!" And with that, he was off and out into the rain.

This eleven-year-old boy walked the streets of the town going door to door and handing everybody he met in the street a gospel tract. After two hours of walking in the rain, he was soaked to the bone but down to his very last tract.

He stopped on a corner and looked for someone to hand a tract to, but the streets were totally deserted. Then he turned toward the first home he saw, walked up the drive to the front door and rang the doorbell, but nobody answered. He rang it again and again, but still no answer.

Finally, this eleven-year-old trooper turned to leave, but something stopped him. Again, he turned to the door and rang the bell and knocked loudly on the door with his fist. He waited, something holding him there on the front porch.

He rang one more time, and this time the door slowly opened. Standing in the doorway was a very sad-looking elderly lady. She softly asked, "What can I do for you son?" With radiant eyes and a smile that lit up her world, the little boy said, "Ma'am, I'm sorry if I disturbed you, but I just want to tell you that Jesus really does love you, and I came to give you my very last gospel tract which will tell you all about Jesus and His great love."

With that, he handed her his last tract, and turned to leave. She called to him as he left. "Thank you, son! And God bless you!" Well, the following Sabbath morning in church, the pastor was in the pulpit. As the service began, he asked, " Does anybody have a testimony or want to say anything?"

Slowly, in the back row of the church, an elderly lady stood to her feet. She said, "No one in this church knows me. I've never been here before.

"You see, before last weekend I was not a Christian. My husband passed on some time ago, leaving me totally alone in this world. Last week, on a particularly cold and rainy day, I felt even more alone and felt I had come to the end of the line where I no longer had any hope or will to live. So I took a rope and a chair and ascended the stairway into the attic of my home.

"I fastened the rope securely to a rafter in the roof, then stood on the chair and fastened the other end of the rope around my neck. Standing on that chair, so lonely and broken-hearted, I was about to leap off, when suddenly the loud ringing of my doorbell downstairs startled me. I thought, "I'll wait a minute, and whoever it is will go away.

"I waited and waited, but the ringing doorbell seemed to get louder and more insistent, and then the person ringing also started knocking

125

loudly. I thought to myself again, 'Who on earth could this be?! Nobody ever rings my bell or comes to see me.'

"I loosened the rope from my neck and started for the front door, all the while the bell rang louder and louder. When I opened the door and looked I could hardly believe my eyes, for there on my front porch was the most radiant and angelic little boy I had ever seen in my life.

"His smile, oh, how could I ever describe it to you! And the words that came from his mouth caused my heart, that had long been dead, to leap to life as he exclaimed with a cherub-like voice, 'Ma'am, I just came to tell you that Jesus really does love you.'

"Then he gave me this gospel tract that I now hold in my hand. As the little angel disappeared back out into the cold and rain, I closed my door and read slowly every word of this. Then I went up to my attic to get my rope and chair. I wouldn't be needing them any more.

"You see, I am now a happy child of the King and since the address of your church was on the back of this gospel tract, I have come here to personally say thank you to God's little angel, who came just in the nick of time, and by so doing spared my soul from hell."

There was not a dry eye in the church. And as shouts of praise and honour to the King resounded off the rafters of the building, the pastor descended from the pulpit to the front pew where the little angel was seated. He took his son in his arms and sobbed uncontrollably. Probably, no church has had a more glorious moment; and probably, this universe has never seen a papa that was more filled with love and honour for his Son.

Except for one. This Father also allowed His Son to go out into a cold and dark world. He received His Son back with unspeakable joy, and as all of heaven shouted praises and honour to the King, the Father sat His beloved Son on a throne, far above all principality and power.

To God be the glory, great things he has done.

# NO ENEMIES

The preacher, in his sermon, used "Forgive your enemies" as his subject. After a long sermon, he asked how many were willing to forgive their enemies. About half held up their hands.

Not satisfied, he harangued for another twenty minutes and repeated his question. This time he received a response of about 80 percent.

Still unsatisfied, he lectured for another 15 minutes and repeated his question. With all thoughts now on dinner, all responded except one elderly lady in the rear. "Mrs. Jones, why are you not willing to forgive your enemies?"
"I don't have any."
"Mrs. Jones, that is very unusual. How old are you?"
"Ninety-three."
"Mrs. Jones, please come down in front and tell the congregation how a person can live to be ninety-three, and not have an enemy in the world."

The little sweetheart of a lady tottered down the aisle, very slowly turned around and said: "It's easy. I just outlived them."

# DANCING WITH JESUS

You dream that you and the Lord Jesus are walking down the road together. For much of the way, the Lord's footprints go along steadily, consistently, rarely varying in pace. But your footprints are a disorganised stream of zigzags, starts, stops, turnarounds, circles, departures, and returns. For much of the way, it seems to go like this, but gradually your footprints come more in line with the Lord's, soon paralleling His consistently. You and Jesus are walking as true friends!

This seems perfect, but then an interesting thing happens: Your footprints that once etched the sand next to Jesus' are now walking precisely in His steps. Inside His larger footprints are your smaller ones; you and Jesus are becoming one.

This goes on for many miles, but gradually you notice another change. The footprints inside the large footprints seem to grow larger. Eventually they disappear altogether. There is only one set of footprints. This goes on for a long time, but suddenly the second set of footprints is back. This time it seems even worse! They zig-zag all over the place. Stop. Start: a variable mess of prints. You are amazed and shocked.

Then your dream ends. So you decided to ask God what the dream meant: "Lord, I understand the first scene, with zigzags and fits. I was a new Christian; I was just learning. But You walked on through the storm and helped me learn to walk with You."
"That is correct."

"And when the smaller footprints were inside of Yours, I was actually learning to walk in Your steps, following You very closely."
"Very good. You have understood everything so far."

"When the smaller footprints grew and filled in Yours, I suppose that I was becoming like You in every way."
"Precisely."

"So, Lord, was there a regression or something? The footprints separated, and this time it was worse than at first."

There is a pause as the Lord answers, with a smile in His voice. "You didn't know? It was then that we danced!"

# SCARRED FOR LIFE

There once was a little girl who had a bad temper. Her mother gave her a bag of nails and told her that every time she lost her temper, she must hammer a nail into the fence.

By the end of the first day the girl had driven 37 nails into the fence. But, over the next few weeks, as she learned to control her anger, the number of nails hammered daily gradually dwindled down. She discovered that it was easier to hold her temper than to drive those nails into the fence.

Finally, the day came when the girl didn't lose her temper at all. She told her mother about it and the mother suggested that the girl now pull out one nail for each day that she was able to hold her temper.

The days passed and soon the young girl was finally able to tell her mother that all the nails were gone. The mother took her daughter by the hand and led her to the fence. "You have done well," she said, "but look at the holes in the fence. The fence will never be the same again. When you say things in anger, they leave a scar just like the nails in the fence."

Remember: A verbal wound can be even worse than a physical one.

# IDENTIFY TO SAVE

*And God became man and dwelt among us*
*(John 1:14)*

There was once a man who didn't believe in God, and he didn't hesitate to let others know how he felt about religion and religious holidays, like Christmas. His wife, however, did believe, and she raised their children to also have faith in God, despite his disparaging comments.

One snowy Christmas Eve, his wife was taking their children to a Christmas Eve service in the farm community in which they lived. She asked him to come, but he refused.

"That story is nonsense!" he said. "Why would God lower Himself to come to Earth as a man? That's ridiculous!" So she and the children left him at home.

A while later, the winds grew stronger and the snow turned into a blizzard. As the man looked out the window, all he saw was a blinding snowstorm. He sat down to relax before the fire for the evening. Then he heard a loud thump. Something had hit the window. Then another thump. He looked out, but couldn't see more than a few feet.

When the snow let up a little, he ventured outside to see what could have been beating on his window. In the field near his house he saw a flock of wild geese. It appeared that they had been flying south for the winter when they got caught in the snowstorm and couldn't go on.

They were lost and stranded on his farm, with no food or shelter. They just flapped their wings and flew around the field in low circles, blindly and aimlessly. A couple of them had flown into his window, it seemed. The man felt sorry for the geese and wanted to help them.

The barn would be a great place for them to stay, he thought. It was warm and safe; surely they could spend the night there and wait out the storm.

So he walked over to the barn and opened the doors wide, then watched and waited, hoping they would notice the open barn and go inside. But the geese just fluttered around aimlessly and didn't seem to notice the barn or realise what it could mean for them. The man tried to get their attention, but that just seemed to scare them and they moved further away. He went into the house and came with some bread, broke it up, and made a breadcrumb trail leading to the barn. They still didn't catch on.

Now he was getting frustrated. He got behind them and tried to shoo them toward the barn, but they only got more scared and scattered in every direction except toward the barn.

Nothing he did could get them to go into the barn where they would be warm and safe.

"Why don't they follow me?!" he exclaimed. "Can't they see this is the only place where they can survive the storm?" He thought for a moment and realised that they just wouldn't follow a human. "If only I were a goose, then I could save them," he said out loud. Then he had an idea. He went into the barn, got one of his own geese, and carried it in his arms as he circled around behind the flock of wild geese. He then released it. His goose flew through the flock and straight into the safety of the barn; and one by one the other geese followed.

He stood silently for a moment as the words he had spoken a few minutes earlier replayed in his mind: "If only I were a goose, then I could save them!" Then he thought about what he had said to his wife earlier. "Why would God want to be like us? That's ridiculous!"

Suddenly it all made sense.

That is what God had done. We were like the geese - blind, lost, perishing. God had His Son become like us so that He could show us the way and save us. It suddenly dawned on him that that was the meaning of Christmas!

As the winds and blinding snow died down, his soul became quiet and pondered this wonderful thought.

He at last understood what Christmas was all about, why Christ had come. Years of doubt and disbelief vanished like the passing storm.   He fell to his knees in the snow, and prayed his first prayer:  "Thank You, God, for coming in human form to get me out of the storm!"

# YOU TOOK MY PLACE

One day, a man went to visit a church. He got there early, parked his car and got out. Another car pulled up near and the driver got out and said, "I always park there! You took my place!"

The visitor went inside for the Bible class, found an empty seat and sat down. A young lady from the church approached him and stated, "That's my seat! You took my place!"

The visitor was somewhat distressed by this rude welcome, but said nothing. After the Bible class, the visitor went into the sanctuary and sat down. Another member walked up to him and said, "That's where I always sit! You took my place!" The visitor was even more troubled by this treatment, but still he said nothing.

Later, as the congregation was praying for Christ to dwell among them, the visitor stood up, and his appearance began to change. Horrible scars became visible on his hands and on his sandaled feet.

Someone from the congregation noticed him and called out, "What happened to you?" The visitor replied, as his hat became a crown of thorns, and a tear fell from his eye, "I took your place."

# GO AND SIN NO MORE

There was a tradesman, a painter named Jack, who was very interested in making a dollar wherever he could. So, he often would thin down his paint to make it go a wee bit further. As it happened, he got away with this for some time.

One day, the local church decided to do a big restoration project. Jack put in a painting bid and, because his price was so competitive, he got the job. And so he started, erecting the trestles and putting up the planks, and buying the paint and thinning it down with turpentine.

Jack was up on the scaffolding, painting away; the job was nearly done, when suddenly there was a horrendous clap of thunder.

The sky opened and the rain poured down, washing the thin paint from all over the church and knocking Jack off the scaffold to land on the lawn.

Jack was no fool. He knew this was a judgment from the Almighty, so he fell on his knees and cried, "Oh, God! Forgive me! What should I do?"

And from the thunder, a mighty voice spoke, "Repaint! Repaint! And thin no more!"

# HAVE YOU TOLD ANYONE LATELY THAT YOU LOVE GOD?

Think back to when you met that man that you just knew would be 'the one'. Remember when you realised and admitted to yourself that you loved him?

Now, remember how much you wanted to act like you were in a movie, and yell to everyone in the football stadium, "I love [fill in the name]!"

You told family and friends how perfect he was. You told them how he was just what you were looking for.

Well, I told The Lord that I love Him today. And He said to me, "How much do you love me?

"You haven't told anyone how good I've been to you. You haven't shared how perfect my love is. "You haven't spread the good news that I am always there to listen to your problems.

"You haven't told your family how I helped you pay your bills when you didn't have a high paying job, or how I got you a better one. You didn't tell your friends and family how I took away that addiction that would have cost you not only your job, but that man who was 'just what you were looking for'.

"So how much do you really love me?"

So, I said I would share with my friends and family (for starters) just how wonderful, perfect, understanding, patient, loving, unselfish, considerate and forgiving God really is.

He has blessed me with a family that loves me and friends that I can confide in. But even more than that, He has saved me from destruction I couldn't even see coming. He gave to me the peace of knowing Him and He has never broken a promise.

Truly He is the best thing that has ever happened to me.

And I stand here today to yell to you all, "I love The Lord!"

When was the last time you told the Lord you love Him?

# GOD WORKS IN A MYSTERIOUS WAY

Sometimes we wonder, "What did I do to deserve this?" or "Why did God have to do this to me?" Here is a wonderful explanation!

A daughter was telling her mother how everything was going wrong: she was failing algebra, her boyfriend broke up with her and her best friend was moving away.

Meanwhile, her mother was baking a cake and asked her daughter if she would like a snack, and the daughter says, "Absolutely mum, I love your cake."

"Here, have some cooking oil," her mother offered. "Yuck," said her daughter.
"How about a couple raw eggs?"
"Gross, mum!"
"Would you like some flour then? Or maybe baking soda?"
"Mum, those are all yucky!"

To which the mother replied: "Yes, all those things seem bad all by themselves. But when they are put together in the right way, they make a wonderfully delicious cake!

God works the same way. Many times we wonder why He would let us go through such bad and difficult times. But God knows that when He puts these things all in His order, they always work for good. We just have to trust Him and, eventually, they will all make something wonderful.

God is crazy about you. He sends you flowers every spring and a sunrise every morning. Whenever you want to talk, He'll listen. He can live anywhere in the universe, yet He chose your heart.

Life may not be the party we hoped for, but while we are here we might as well dance.

*All things work together for good to them that love the Lord (Romans 8:28)*

# SELF REALISATION –
# HAPPINESS BEGINS WITH
# YOU

A time comes in your life when you finally get it -
when, in the midst of all your fears and insanity,
you stop dead in your tracks and somewhere the
voice inside your head cries out, "ENOUGH!"

Enough fighting and crying, or struggling to hold
on. And, like a child quietening down after a
blind tantrum, your sobs begin to subside; you
shudder once or twice, you blink back your tears
and begin to look at the world through new eyes.
This is your awakening.

You realise it's time to stop hoping and waiting
for something to change, or for happiness,
safety and security to come galloping over the
next horizon.

You come to terms with the fact that you are
neither Prince Charming nor Cinderella. And
that, in the real world, there aren't always fairy-
tale endings (or beginnings, for that matter). And
that any guarantee of "happily ever after" must
begin with you - and in the process, a sense of
serenity is born of acceptance.

You awaken to the fact that you are not perfect
and that not everyone will always love,

appreciate, or approve of who or what you are - and that's okay.

You learn the importance of loving and championing yourself - and in the process, a sense of newfound confidence is born of self-approval.

You stop complaining and blaming other people for the things they did to you (or didn't do for you) and you learn that the only thing you can really count on is the unexpected.

You learn that people don't always say what they mean or mean what they say; that not everyone will always be there for you; that it's not always about you. So you learn to stand on your own and to take care of yourself - and in the process, a sense of safety and security is born of self-reliance.

You stop judging and pointing fingers and you begin to accept people as they are and overlook their shortcomings and human frailties - and in the process, a sense of peace and contentment is born of forgiveness.

You realise that much of the way you view yourself and the world around you is as a result of all the messages and opinions that have been ingrained into your psyche. You begin to sift through all the junk you've been fed about how you should behave, how you should look, how much you should weigh, what you should wear, what you should do for a living, how much money you should make, what you should drive, how and where you should live, who you should marry, the importance of having and raising children, and what you owe your parents, family and friends.

You learn to open up to new worlds and different points of view. And you begin reassessing and redefining who you are and what you really stand for.

You learn the difference between wanting and needing and you begin to discard the doctrines and values you've outgrown, or should never have bought into, to begin with - and in the process, you learn to go with your instincts.

You learn that it is truly in giving that we receive. And that there is power and glory in creating and contributing. You stop manoeuvring through life merely as a "consumer" looking for your next fix.

Then you learn about love: how to love, how much to give in love, when to stop giving and when to walk away.

You learn to look at relationships as they really are and not as you would have them be.

You stop trying to control people, situations and outcomes.

And you learn that alone does not mean lonely.

You stop working so hard at putting your feelings aside, smoothing things over and ignoring your needs.
You learn that feelings of entitlement are perfectly okay, and that it is your right to want things and to ask for the things you want - and that sometimes it is necessary to make demands.

You come to the realisation that you deserve to be treated with love, kindness, sensitivity and respect - and that you won't settle for less.
You learn that your body really is a temple - you begin to care for it and treat it with respect. You begin to eat a balanced diet, drink more water, and take more time to exercise.

You learn that being tired fuels doubt, fear and uncertainty, and so you take more time to rest. And, just as food fuels the body, laughter fuels our soul. So you take more time to laugh and play.

You learn that, for the most part, you get in life what you believe you deserve - and that much of life truly is a self-fulfilling prophecy. You learn that anything worth achieving is worth working for, and that wishing for something to happen is different from working toward making it happen. More importantly, you learn that in order to achieve success you need direction, discipline, and perseverance.

You learn that no one can do it all alone, and that it's okay to risk asking for help.

You learn that the only thing you must truly fear is the greatest robber baron of all: fear itself. You learn to step right into and through your fears, because you know that whatever happens you can handle it and to give into fear is to give away the right to live life on your own terms. You learn to fight for your life and not to squander it living under a cloud of impending doom.

Slowly, you begin to take responsibility for yourself, by yourself, and you make yourself a promise to never betray yourself and to never, ever settle for less than what is true and right.

And you make a point to keep smiling, to keep trusting, and to stay open to every wonderful possibility.

Finally, with courage in your heart and God by your side, you take a stand, you take a deep breath, and you begin to live as best you can, the life God wants you to live.

# TAPESTRY OF LIFE

As I faced my Maker at the last judgment, I knelt before the Lord along with all the other souls.

Before each of us laid our lives, like the squares of a quilt in many piles. An angel sat before each of us, sewing our quilt squares together into a tapestry that is our life.

But as my angel took each piece of cloth off the pile, I noticed how ragged and empty each of the squares were - they were filled with giant holes. Each square was labeled with a part of my life that had been difficult; the challenges and temptations I was faced with in everyday life. I saw hardships that I endured, which were the largest holes of all.

I glanced around me. Nobody else had such squares. Other than a tiny hole here and there, the other tapestries were filled with rich color and the bright hues of worldly fortune.

I gazed upon my own life and was disheartened. My angel was sewing the ragged pieces of cloth together, threadbare and empty, like binding air.

Finally, the time came when each life was to be displayed, held up to the light, the scrutiny of truth.

The others rose, each in turn, holding up their tapestries. So filled their lives had been.

My angel looked at me, and nodded for me to rise. My gaze dropped to the ground in shame.

I hadn't had all the earthly fortunes. I had love in my life, and laughter. But there had also been trials of illness, and death, and false accusations that took from me my world, as I knew it.

I had to start over many times. I often struggled with the temptation to quit, only to somehow muster the strength to pick up and begin again. I spent many nights on my knees in prayer, asking for help and guidance in my life.

I had often been held up to ridicule, which I endured painfully, each time offering it up to the Father in hopes that I would not melt within my skin, beneath the judgmental gaze of those who unfairly judged me.

And now, I had to face the truth. My life was what it was, and I had to accept it. I rose and slowly lifted the combined squares of my life to the light.

An awe-filled gasp filled the air.

I gazed around at the others who stared at me with wide eyes. Then, I looked upon the tapestry before me.

Light flooded the many holes, creating an image: *the face of Christ.*

Then our Lord stood before me, with warmth and love in His eye. He said, "very time you gave over your life to Me, it became My life, My hardships and My struggles.

Each point of light in your life is when you stepped aside and let Me shine through, until there was more of Me than there was of you."

May all our quilts be threadbare and worn, allowing Christ to shine through.

# IN HIS HANDS

A cricket bat in my hands is worth a couple of runs.
A cricket bat in Brian Lara's hands is a world record.
It depends whose hands it's in.

A baseball in my hands is worth about £3.
A baseball in Mark McGwire's hands is worth £10 million.
It depends whose hands it's in.

A tennis racket is useless in my hands.
A tennis racket in Serena Williams' hands is a Championship trophy.
It depends whose hands it's in.

A rod in my hands will keep away a wild animal.
A rod in Moses' hands will part the mighty sea.
It depends whose hands it's in.

A slingshot in my hands is a kid's toy.
A slingshot in David's hand is a mighty weapon.
It depends whose hands it's in.

Two fish and 5 loaves of bread in my hands are a couple of fish sandwiches.
Two fish and 5 loaves of bread in God's hands will feed thousands.
It depends whose hands it's in.

Nails in my hands might produce a birdhouse.
Nails in Jesus Christ's hands will produce
salvation for the entire world.
It depends whose hands it's in.

So put your concerns, your worries, your fears,
your hopes, your dreams, your families and your
relationships in God's hands.

# JESUS PAID THE PRICE

There once was a man named George Thomas, who was a pastor in a small Yorkshire town. One Easter Sunday morning he came to the church carrying a rusty, bent, old bird cage, and set it by the pulpit. Eyebrows were raised and, as if in response, Pastor Thomas began to speak. "I was walking through town yesterday, when I saw a young boy coming toward me swinging this bird cage. On the bottom of the cage were three little wild birds, shivering with cold and fright. I stopped the lad and asked, 'What you got there, son?'"

"Just some old birds," came the reply.

"What are you gonna do with them?" I asked.

"Take 'em home and have fun with 'em," he answered. "I'm gonna tease 'em and pull out their feathers to make 'em fight. I'm gonna have a real good time."

"But you'll get tired of those birds sooner or later. What will you do then?"

"Oh, I got some cats," said the little boy, "They like birds. I'll take 'em to them."

The pastor was silent for a moment. "How much do you want for those birds, son?"

"Huh? Why, you don't want them birds, mister. They're just plain old-field birds. They don't sing. They ain't even pretty!"

"How much?" the pastor asked again.

The boy sized up the pastor as if he were crazy and said, "£10?"

The pastor reached in his pocket and took out a ten-pound note. He placed it in the boy's hand, and in a flash, the boy was gone.

The pastor picked up the cage and gently carried it to the end of the alley where there was a tree and a grassy spot. Setting the cage down, he opened the door, and by softly tapping the bars persuaded the birds out, setting them free.

Well, that explained the empty birdcage on the pulpit, and then the pastor began to tell this story.

"One day Satan and Jesus were having a conversation. Satan had just come from the Garden of Eden, and he was gloating and boasting. 'Yes, sir, I just caught the world full of people down there. Set me a trap, used bait I knew they couldn't resist. Got 'em all!'

'What are you going to do with them?' Jesus asked.

Satan replied, 'Oh, I'm gonna have fun! I'm gonna teach them how to marry and divorce each other, how to hate and abuse each other, how to drink and smoke and curse. I'm gonna teach them how to invent guns and bombs and kill each other. I'm really gonna have fun!'

'And what will you do when you're finished with them?' Jesus asked.

'Oh, I'll kill 'em,' Satan glared proudly.

"How much do you want for them?" Jesus asked.

'Oh, you don't want those people. They ain't no good. Why, you'll take them and they'll just hate you. They'll spit on you, curse you and kill you. You don't want those people!'

'How much?' Jesus asked again.

Satan looked at Jesus and sneered, 'All your blood, tears and your life.'

Jesus said, 'Done!'

"Then He paid the price."

The pastor picked up the cage and he walked from the pulpit.

# CHRIST IS EVERYWHERE

One particular day, Sally walked into the seminary and knew they were in for a fun day.

On the wall was a big target and on a nearby table were many darts. Dr. Smith, her teacher, told the students to draw a picture of someone that they disliked or someone who had made them angry, and he would allow them to throw darts at the person's picture.

Sally's friend drew a picture of the girl who had stolen her boyfriend. Another friend drew a picture of his little brother. Sally drew a picture of a former friend, putting a great deal of detail into her drawing, even drawing pimples on the face. Sally was pleased with the overall effect she had achieved.

The class lined up and began throwing darts. Some of the students threw their darts with such force that their targets were ripping apart.

Sally looked forward to her turn, and was filled with disappointment when Dr. Smith, because of time limits, asked the students to return to their seats. As Sally sat thinking about how angry she was because she didn't have a chance to throw any darts at her target. Dr. Smith began removing the target from the wall.

Underneath the target was a picture of Jesus. A hush fell over the room as each student viewed the mangled picture of Jesus; holes and jagged marks covered His face and His eyes were pierced.

Dr. Smith said only these words; "In as much as ye have done it unto the least of these my brethren, ye have done it unto Me." (Matthew 25:40)

No other words were necessary. The tear-filled eyes of the students focused only on the picture of Christ.

# PRAY FOR ONE ANOTHER

A voyaging ship was wrecked during a storm at sea, and only two of the men on it were able to swim to a small, desert-like island.

The two survivors, not knowing what else to do, agreed that they had no other resource but to pray to God. However, to find out whose prayer was more powerful, they agreed to divide the territory between them and stay on opposite sides of the island.

The first thing they prayed for was food.

The next morning, the first man saw a fruit-bearing tree on his side of the island, and he was able to eat its fruit. The other man's parcel of land remained barren.

After a week, the first man became lonely and he decided to pray for a wife. The next day, another ship was wrecked, and the only survivor was a woman who swam to his side of the land. On the other side of the island, there was nothing.

Soon the first man prayed for a house, clothes and more food. The next day, like magic, all of these were given to him. However, the second man still had nothing.

Finally, the first man prayed for a ship, so that he and his wife could leave the island. In the morning he found a ship docked at his side of the island. The first man boarded the ship with his wife and decided to leave the second man on the island. He considered the other man unworthy to receive God's blessings, since none of his prayers had been answered.

As the ship was about to leave, the first man heard a voice from heaven booming, "Why are you leaving your companion on the island?"

"My blessings are mine alone, since I was the one who prayed for them," the first man answered. "His prayers were all unanswered and so he does not deserve anything."

"You are mistaken!" the voice rebuked him. "He had only one prayer, which I answered. If not for that, you would not have received any of my blessings."

"Tell me," the first man asked the voice, "what did he pray for that I should owe him anything?" "He prayed that all your prayers be answered."

*** 

For all we know, our blessings are not the fruits of our prayers alone, but those of another praying for us.

With obedience comes blessings.
My prayer for you today, is that all sincere prayers are answered.

# HOW HEAVY IS A PRAYER?

A poorly dressed lady, with a look of defeat on her face, walked into a corner shop. She approached the owner of the store in a most humble manner, and asked if he would let her charge a few groceries.

She softly explained that her husband was unable to work, they had seven children and they needed food, the grocer, scoffed at her and requested that she leave his store. Realising the family needs, she said: "Please, sir! I will bring you the money just as soon as I can." The grocer told her he could not give her credit, as she did not have a charge account at his store.

Standing beside the counter was a customer who overheard the conversation between the two. The customer walked forward and told the grocer that he would stand good for whatever she needed for her family.

The grocer said in a very reluctant voice, "Do you have a grocery list?"
"Yes sir."
"Okay," he said. "Put your grocery list on the scales and whatever your grocery list weighs, I will give you that amount in groceries." The lady hesitated a moment, then with a bowed head, she reached into her purse and took out a piece of paper and scribbled something on it. She then

laid the piece of paper on the scale carefully, with her head still bowed.

The eyes of the grocer and the customer showed amazement when the scales went down and stayed down.

The grocer, staring at the scales, turned slowly to the customer and said begrudgingly, "I can't believe it."

The customer smiled and the grocer started putting the groceries on the other side of the scales. The scale did not balance. So he continued to put more and more groceries on them until the scales would hold no more. The grocer stood there in utter disgust.

Finally, he grabbed the piece of paper from the scales and looked at it with greater amazement.

It was not a grocery list. It was a prayer that said: "Dear Lord, you know my needs and I am leaving this in your hands".

The grocer gave her the groceries that he had gathered and stood in stunned silence. The lady thanked him and left the store.

The customer handed a twenty-pound note to the grocer and said, "It was worth every penny of it."

Only God knows how much a prayer weighs.

# PRAYERS

# PRAYERS OPEN DOORS

I asked the Lord to bless you
As I prayed for you today
To guide you and protect you
As you go along your way
His love is always with you
His promises are true,
And when we give Him all our cares,
You know He'll see us through
So when the road you're travelling on
Seems difficult at best,
Just remember, prayers open doors,
And God will do the rest.

# PRAYER SEEDS

*1 Thessalonians 5:25: Brothers [and sisters], pray for us.*

Father, we thank you for life – that we are able to breathe, even though some of us find even that hard at times.

We thank you Father for providing for us in the various ways that You do. You know our needs more than we do.

We recognise that we should not worry about the things that we have no control over, but being human, we worry, panic, moan when we cannot see the way ahead clearly enough.

But we are still thankful that You give us the Scriptures and one another to induce confidence in You, in Your abiding presence, in all situations that we find ourselves.

The life we now live is but temporary; but help us to start to appreciate eternal life, now, even now.

Please continue to support us, directly and through our associates, as we make use of the opportunities we have: to help and to accept help; to give and to receive; to empathise and to accept empathy; to love and to be loved.

As each day passes, may it leave behind us having a stronger faith in you, so that during the light we can give thanks and in the inevitable twilight and darkness we will find that iron rail in you, for sterling support.

And so, Father, we look around, we see, we hear the requests for prayers, and we now respond. As a congregation, we sow our prayer seeds for:

- Those we know who are ill
- Those who know they are ill but are unable to say so
- Those who are ill but do not know it
- Those among us who grieve for the loss of loved ones.

We sow our prayer seeds also for:

- The many young people who do silly things before they think
- The innocent children who are abused
- The elderly who are taken advantaged of.

We pray too for:
- The families that are wrecked because of wars
- The parents, spouses and children of soldiers who have died in these wars and suicide bombings

- The governments who are charged with the responsibility to administer a just society
- Those who do evil, and scheme to destroy the innocent

And finally, for now, we pray that Your ministering influence will be with those who share with us Your Word.

In all our thanks and requests we pray, in the name of Jesus, that Your will be done on Earth as it is in heaven.

Amen

*Albert A. C. Waite*
Newbold Family Church Service
11 October 2003

# BLESSINGS...

You may be going through a tough time right now but God is getting ready to bless you in a way that only He can.

This prayer is powerful, and prayer is one of the best gifts we have received. There is no cost but a lot of rewards. Let's continue to pray for one another.

***

Father, I ask You to bless my friends, relatives and email buddies reading this right now. Show them a new revelation of Your love and power.

Holy Spirit, I ask You to minister to their spirit at this very moment.

Where there is pain, give them Your peace and mercy. Where there is self-doubt, release a renewed confidence through Your grace.

Bless their homes, families, finances, their goings and their comings.

In Jesus' precious name.

Amen.

# RELAX AND HUMBLE

Relax your mind and humble your heart to focus on Christ. Allow God to be the only person on your mind while you read this prayer. Friends that pray together, stay together.

Dear Lord, I thank You for this day. I thank You for my being able to see and to hear. I'm blessed because You are a forgiving God and an understanding God. You have done so much for me and You keep on blessing me.

Forgive me this day for everything I have done, said or thought that was not pleasing to you. I ask now for Your forgiveness.

Please keep me safe from all danger and harm. Help me to start each day with a new attitude and plenty of gratitude. Let me make the best of each and every day to clear my mind so that I can hear from You.

Please broaden my mind that I can accept all good things. Let me not whine and whimper over things I have no control over. Let me continue to see sin through Your eyes and acknowledge it as evil. And when I sin, let me repent, and confess with my mouth my wrongdoing, and receive Your forgiveness.

And when this world closes in on me, let me remember Jesus' example - to slip away and find a quiet place to pray. It's the best response when I'm pushed beyond my limits. I know that when I can't pray, You listen to my heart.

Continue to use me to do Your will.
Continue to bless me so that I may be a blessing to others. Keep me strong so that I may help the weak. Keep me uplifted so that I may have words of encouragement for others. I pray for those who are lost and can't find their way. I pray for those who are misjudged and misunderstood. I pray for those who don't know You intimately. I pray for those who don't believe. But I thank you that I believe.

I believe that God changes people and God changes things. I pray for all my sisters and brothers. For each and every family member in their households. I pray for peace, love and joy in their homes; that they are out of debt and all their needs are met.

I pray that everyone that reads or hear this prayer knows there is no problem, circumstance or situation greater than God. Every battle is in Your hands for You to fight. I pray that these words be received into the hearts of every eye that sees them and every mouth that confesses them willingly.

This is my prayer in Jesus' name,
Amen.

# IN JESUS' NAME

Father, I ask you to bless the person who is reading this right now. I am asking You to minister to their spirit at this very moment.

Where there is pain, give them Your peace and mercy. Where there is self-doubting, release a renewed confidence in Your ability to work through them.

Where there is tiredness or exhaustion, I ask You to give them understanding, patience and strength, as they learn submission to your leading.

Where there is spiritual stagnation, I ask You to renew them by revealing Your nearness, and by drawing them into greater intimacy with You. Where there is fear, reveal Your love and release to them Your courage.

Where there is a sin blocking them, reveal it and break its hold over their life.

Bless their finances, give them greater vision, and raise up leaders and friends to support and encourage them.

Give them discernment to recognise the evil forces around them, and reveal to them the power they have in You to defeat these forces. I ask You to do these things in Jesus' name. Amen

# BLESS THOSE IN MY ADDRESS BOOK TOO

Every single evening
As I'm lying here in bed,
This tiny little prayer
Keeps running through my head.

God bless all my family
Wherever they may be,
Keep them warm and safe from harm
For they're so close to me.

And God, there is one more thing
I wish that you could do,
Hope You don't mind me asking
Please bless my computer too.

Now I know that it's unusual
To bless a motherboard,
But listen just a second
While I explain it to you, Lord.

You see that little metal box
Holds more than odds and ends,
Inside those small compartments
Rest so many of my friends.

I know so much about them
By the kindness that they give,
And this little scrap of metal
Takes me in to where they live.

By faith is how I know them
Much the same as You,
We share in what life brings us
And from that our friendships grew.

Please take an extra minute
From your duties up above,
To bless those in my address book
That's filled with so much love.

Wherever else this prayer may reach
To each and every friend,
To those who read and share it;
To them your blessings send.

Amen

# TIME FOR GOD

God, when I received this mail, I thought,
'I don't have time for this, and, this is really
inappropriate during work.'

Then I realised that this kind of thinking is
exactly what has caused lot of the problems in
our world today.

We try to keep God in church on worship days,
and, the unlikely event of a midweek service.

We do like to have Him around during sickness
and, of course, at funerals.  However, we don't
have time, or room, for Him during work or play,
because that's the part of our lives we think we
can, and should, handle on our own.

May God forgive me for ever thinking that there
is a time or place where He is not to be first in
my life.

Amen.

# REALITY

The Lord is my Shepherd
*That's relationship*

I shall not want
*That's supply*

He makes me to lie down in green pastures
*That's rest*

He leads me beside the still waters
*That's refreshment*

He restores my soul
*That's healing*

He leads me in the paths of righteousness
*That's guidance*

For His name sake
*That's purpose*

Yes, though I walk through the valley of the
shadow of death
*That's testing*

I will fear no evil
*That's protection*


For You are with me

*That's faithfulness*

Your rod and Your staff they comfort me
*That's discipline*

You prepare a table before me in the presence
of mine enemies
*That's hope*

You anoint my head with oil
*That's consecration*

My cup runs over
*That's abundance*

Surely goodness and mercy shall follow me all
the days of my life
*That's blessing*

And I will dwell in the house of the Lord
*That's security*

Forever
*That's Eternity*

Face it, the Lord is crazy about you.

# POEMS

# ASAP

Ever wonder about the abbreviation ASAP?
Generally, we think of it in terms of hurry and
stress in our lives. Perhaps if we think of this
abbreviation in a different manner, we will begin
to find a new way to deal with those rough
days...

\*\*\*

There's work to do, deadlines to meet;
You've got no time to spare.
But as you hurry and scurry -
ALWAYS SAY A PRAYER

In the midst of family chaos,
"Quality time" is rare.
Do your best; let God do the rest -
ALWAYS SAY A PRAYER.

It may seem like your worries
Are more than you can bear.
Slow down and take a breather -
ALWAYS SAY A PRAYER

God knows how stressful life is;
He wants to ease our cares,
And He'll respond to all your needs
ALWAYS SAY A PRAYER.

ASAP - ALWAYS SAY A PRAYER.

# GOD PAID YOUR BILL

As I was walking down life's highway
Many years ago,
I came upon a sign that read
Heavens Grocery Store.

When I got a little closer
The doors swung open wide,
And when I came to myself
I was standing inside.
I saw a host of angels
They were standing everywhere.
One handed me a basket and said,
"My child shop with care."

Everything a human needed
Was in that grocery store,
And what you could not carry
You could come back for more.
First I got some patience
Love was in that same row.
Further down was understanding
You need that everywhere you go.

I got a box or two of wisdom
And faith a bag or two.
And charity of course,
I would need some of that too.
I couldn't miss the Holy Ghost,
It was all over the place;
And then some strength and courage

To help me run this race.
My basket was getting full
But I remembered I needed grace.

And then I chose salvation,
For salvation was for free.
I tried to get enough of that
To do for you and me.

Then I started to the counter
To pay my grocery bill,
For I thought I had everything
To do the Masters will.

As I went up the aisle
I saw prayer and put that in.
For I knew when I stepped outside
I would run into sin.

Peace and Joy were plentiful,
The last things on the shelf.
Song and praise were hanging near,
So I just helped myself.

Then I said to the angel,
"Now how much do I owe?"
She smiled and said, "Just take them
everywhere you go."

Again I asked, "Really now,
"How much do I owe?"
"My child" he said, "God paid your bill
A long, long time ago."

# JIM CHECKING IN

A priest passing through his church
In the middle of the day.
Decided to pause by the altar
And see who had come to pray.

Just then the back door opened,
A man came down the aisle.
The priest frowned as he saw
The man hadn't shaved in a while.

His shirt was kind of shabby
And his coat was worn and frayed.
The man knelt, he bowed his head,
Then rose and walked away.

In the days that followed,
Each noontime came this chap;
Each time he knelt just for a moment,
A lunch pail in his lap.

Well, the priest's suspicions grew,
With robbery a main fear,
He decided to stop the man and ask him,
"What are you doing here?"

The old man said, he worked down the road.
Lunch was half an hour.
Lunchtime was his prayer time,
For finding strength and power.

"I stay only moments, see,
Because the factory is so far away;
As I kneel here talking to the Lord,
This is kind of what I say:

"I just came again to tell you, Lord,
How happy I've been,
Since we found each other's friendship
And you took away my sin.

"Don't know much of how to pray,
But I think about you everyday.
So, Jesus, this is Jim
Checking in today."

The priest feeling foolish,
Told Jim, that was fine.
He told the man he was welcome
To come and pray just anytime.

Time to go, Jim smiled, and said
"Thanks." He hurried to the door.
The priest knelt at the altar,
He'd never done it before.

His cold heart melted, warmed with love,
And met with Jesus there.
As the tears flowed, in his heart,
He repeated old Jim's prayer:

"I just came again to tell you, Lord,
How happy I've been,
Since we found each other's friendship
And you took away my sin.

"I don't know much of how to pray,
But I think about you everyday.
So, Jesus, this is me
Checking in today."

Past noon one day, the priest noticed
That old Jim hadn't come.
As more days passed without Jim,
He began to worry some.

At the factory, he asked about him,
Learning he was ill.
The hospital staff were worried,
But he'd given them a thrill.

The week that Jim was with them,
Brought changes in the ward.
His smiles, a joy contagious.
Changed people, were his reward.

The head nurse couldn't understand
When no flowers, calls or cards came,
Not a visitor he had.

The priest stayed by his bed,
He voiced the nurse's concern:
No friends came to show they cared.
He had nowhere to turn.

Looking surprised, old Jim spoke up
And with a winsome smile;
"The nurse is wrong, she couldn't know,
That in here all the while

Everyday at noon He's here;
A dear friend of mine, you see.
He sits right down, takes my hand,
Leans over and says to me:

"I just come again to tell you, Jim,
How happy I have been,
Since we found this friendship,
And I took away your sin.

Always love to hear you pray,
I think about you each day,
And so Jim, this is Jesus, checking in today."

# 'VALUE QUOTIENT'

To realise the value of a sister
Ask someone who doesn't have one.
To realise the value of ten years:
Ask a newly divorced couple.

To realise the value of four years:
Ask a graduate.
To realise the value of one year:
Ask a student who has failed a final exam.

To realise the value of nine months:
Ask a mother who gave birth to a stillborn.
To realise the value of one month:
Ask a mother who has given birth to a premature
baby.

To realise the value of one week:
Ask an editor of a weekly newspaper.
To realise the value of one hour:
Ask the lovers who are waiting to meet.

To realise the value of one minute:
Ask a person who has missed the train, bus or
plane.
To realise the value of one-second:
Ask a person who has survived an accident.

To realise the value of one millisecond:
Ask the person who has won a silver medal in
the Olympics.

Time waits for no one. Treasure every moment
you have.
You will treasure it even more when you can
share it with someone special.

To realise the value of a friend:
Lose one.

"When one life shines, the life next to it will
catch the light."

# M4 MOTORWAY

A drunken man in a mobile home
Hugged the lane on the right
That caused the six-car pileup
On the M4 that night.

When broken bodies lay about
And blood was everywhere,
The sirens screamed out elegies,
For death was in the air.

A mother, trapped inside her car,
Was heard above the noise;
Her plaintive plea near split the air:
"Oh, God, please spare my boys!"

She fought to loose her pinned hands;
She struggled to get free,
But mangled metal held her fast
In grim captivity.

Her frightened eyes then focused
On where the back seat once had been,
But all she saw was broken glass and
Two children's seats crushed in.

Her twins were nowhere to be seen;
She did not hear them cry,
And then she prayed they'd been thrown free,
"Oh, God, don't let them die!"

Then firemen came and cut her loose,
But when they searched the back,
They found therein no little boys,
But the seat belts were intact.

They thought the woman had gone mad
And was travelling alone,
But when they turned to question her,
They discovered she was gone.

Policemen saw her running wild
And screaming above the noise
In beseeching supplication,
"Please help me find my boys!

They're four years old and wear blue shirts;
Their jeans are blue to match."
One cop spoke up, "They're in my car,
And they don't have a scratch.

"They said their daddy put them there
And gave them each a cone,
Then told them both to wait for mom
To come and take them home.

"I've searched the area high and low,
But I can't find their dad.
He must have fled the scene,
I guess, and that is very bad."

The mother hugged the twins and said,
While wiping at a tear,
"He could not flee the scene, you see,
For he's been dead a year."

The cop just looked confused and asked,
"Now, how can that be true?"
The boys said, "Mommy, it was a stranger,
He left us to look for you.

"He told us not to worry
And that you would be all right,
And then he put us in this car with
The pretty, flashing light.

"We wanted him to stay with us,
Because he was so kind,
But Mommy, he just hugged us tight
And said you he had to find.

"He said someday we'd understand
And told us not to fuss,
And he said to tell you, Mommy,
He's watching over us."

The mother knew without a doubt
That what they spoke was true,
For she recalled God's sacred Words,
"I will watch over you."

The firemen's notes could not explain
The twisted, mangled car,
And how the three of them escaped
Without a single scar.

But on the cop's report was scribbled,
In print that looks like spray,
'An angel walked the beat tonight
On the M4 motorway.'

# I PRAYED FOR YOU

This morning when I awoke
And saw the sun above,
I softly said, "Good morning, Lord,
Bless everyone I love."

And right away I thought of you
And said a loving prayer,
That He would bless you specially,
And keep you free from care.

I thought of all the happiness
A day could hold in store,
I wished it all for you because
No one deserves it more.

# AROUND THE CORNER

Around the corner I have a friend,
In this great city that has no end.
Yet the days go by and weeks rush on,
And before I know it, a year is gone.

And I never see my old friend's face,
For life is a swift and terrible race,
He knows I like him just as well
As in the days when I rang his bell.

And he rang mine but we were younger then,
And now we are busy, tired men.
Tired of playing a foolish game,
Tired of trying to make a name.

"Tomorrow," I say, "I will call on Jim
Just to show that I'm thinking of him."
But tomorrow comes and tomorrow goes,
And the distance between us grows and grows.

Around the corner, yet miles away,
"Here's a telegram sir, Jim died today."
And that's what we get and deserve in the end.
Around the corner, a vanished friend.

\*\*\*

Remember to stay close to your family and
friends, for they helped make you the person
that you are today.

# THE ROSE IN SPRING

Some say love, it is a river
That drowns the tender reed.
Some say love, it is a razor
That leaves your soul to bleed.
Some say love, it is a hunger,
An endless aching need.
I say love, it is a flower,
And you it's only seed.

It's the heart, afraid of breaking,
That never learns to dance.
It's the dream, afraid of waking,
That never takes a chance.
It's the one who won't be taken,
Who cannot seem to give.
And the soul, afraid of dyin',
That never learns to live.

When the night has been too lonely,
And the road has been too long,
And you think that love is only
For the lucky and the strong,
Just remember in the winter
Far beneath the bitter snows,
Lies the seed, that with the sun's love,
In the spring becomes the rose.

# RED ROSES FOR A LIFETIME

Red roses were her favourites, her name was
also Rose.
And every year her husband sent them, tied with
pretty bows.

The year he died, the roses were delivered to her
door.
The card said, "Be my Valentine," like all the
years before.

Each year he sent her roses, and the note would
always say,
"I love you even more this year, than last year on
this day.

"My love for you will always grow, with every
passing year."
She knew this was the last time that the roses
would appear.

She thought, he ordered roses in advance
before this day.
Her loving husband did not know, that he would
pass away.

He always liked to do things early, way before
the time.
Then, if he got too busy, everything would work
out fine.

She trimmed the stems and placed them in a very special vase.
Then, sat the vase beside the portrait of his smiling face.

She would sit for hours, in her husband's favourite chair.
While staring at his picture, and the roses sitting there.

A year went by, and it was hard to live without her mate;
With loneliness and solitude, which had become her fate.

Then, the very hour, as on many Valentines before,
The doorbell rang, and there were roses sitting by her door.

She brought the roses in, and then just looked at them in shock.
Then, went to get the telephone, to call the florist shop.

The owner answered, and she asked him, if he would explain,
Why would someone do this to her, causing her such pain?

"I know your husband passed away, more than a year ago,"

The owner said, "I knew you'd call, and you would want to know.

The flowers you received today, were paid for in advance.
Your husband always planned ahead, he left nothing to chance.

There is a standing order that I have on file down here,
And he has paid, well in advance, you'll get them every year.

There also is another thing, that I think you should know,
He wrote a special little card, he did this years ago.

Then, should ever I find out that he's no longer here, that's the card that should be sent to you the following year."

She thanked him and hung up the phone, her tears now flowing hard.
Her fingers shaking, as she slowly reached to get the card.

Inside the card, she saw that he had written her a note.
Then, as she stared in total silence, this is what he wrote...

"Hello my love, I know it's been a year since I've been gone.
I hope it hasn't been too hard for you to overcome.

I know it must be lonely, and the pain is very real.
Or if it was the other way, I know how I would feel.

The love we shared made everything so beautiful in life.
I loved you more than words can say, you were the perfect wife.

You were my friend and lover, you fulfilled my every need.
I know it's only been a year, but please try not to grieve.

I want you to be happy, even when you shed your tears.
That is why the roses will be sent to you for many years.

When you get these roses, think of all the happiness,
That we had together, and how both of us were blessed.

I have always loved you and I know I always will.
But, my love, you must go on, you have so much living to do still.

Please, try to find happiness, while living out
your days.
I know it is not easy, but I hope you find some
ways.

The roses will come every year, and they will only
stop,
When your door's not answered, when the florist
stops to knock.

He will come five times that day, in case you
have gone out.
But after his last visit, he will know without a
doubt

To take the roses to the place, where I've
instructed him.
And place the roses where we are, together once
again."

***

Sometimes in life, you find a special friend;
Someone who changes your life just by being
part of it.
Someone who makes you laugh until you can't
stop;
Someone who makes you believe that there
really is good in the world.
Someone who convinces you that there really is
an unlocked door just waiting for you to open it.
This is your Forever Friend.

# IF I KNEW

If I knew it would be the last time
That I'd see you fall asleep,
I would tuck you in more tightly
And pray the Lord, your soul to keep.

If I knew it would be the last time
That I'd see you walk out the door,
I would give you a hug and kiss
And call you back for one more.

If I knew it would be the last time
I'd hear your voice lifted up in praise,
I would videotape each action and word,
So I could play them back day after day.

If I knew it would be the last time,
I could spare an extra minute
To stop and say, "I love you,"
Instead of assuming you know I do.

If I knew it would be the last time
I would be there to share your day,
Well, I'm sure you'll have so many more,
So I can let just this one slip away.

For surely there's always tomorrow
To make up for an oversight,
And we always get a second chance
To make everything just right.

There will always be another day
To say "I love you,"
And certainly there's another chance
To say, "Anything I can do?"

But just in case I might be wrong,
And today is all I get,
I'd like to say how much I love you
And I hope we never forget.

Tomorrow is not promised to anyone,
Young or old alike,
And today may be the last chance
You get to hold your loved one tight.

So if you're waiting for tomorrow,
Why not do it today?
For if tomorrow never comes,
You'll surely regret the day,

That you didn't take that extra time
For a smile, a hug or kiss
And you were too busy to grant someone,
What turned out to be their one last wish.

So hold your loved ones close today,
And whisper in their ear,
Tell them how much you love them
And that you'll always hold them dear.

Take time to say, "I'm sorry,"
"Please forgive me," "Thank you," or "It's okay."
And if tomorrow never comes,
You'll have no regrets about today.

# ALPHABET ROAD TO ZION

*A*lthough things are not perfect

*B*ecause of trial or pain

*C*ontinue in thanksgiving

*D*o not begin to blame

*E*ven when the times are hard

*F*ierce winds are bound to blow

*G*od is forever able

*H*old on to what you know

*I*magine life without His love

*J*oy would cease to be

*K*eep thanking Him for all the things

*L*ove imparts to you

*M*ove out of "Camp Complaining"

*N*o weapon that is known

*O*n earth can yield the power

*P*raise can do alone

*Q*uit looking at the future

*R*edeem the time at hand

*S*tart every day with worship

*T*o "thank" is a command

*U*ntil we see Him coming

*V*ictorious in the sky

*W*e'll run the race with gratitude

*X*alting God most high

*Y*es, there'll be good era and yes some will be bad, but...

*Z*ion waits in glory, where none are ever sad!

# LET IT GO

When people can walk away from you let them walk. Your destiny is never tied to anybody that left. The Bible said that "they came out from us that it might be made manifest that they were not for us. For had they been of us, no doubt they would have continued with us." [1 John 2:19]

People leave you because they are not joined to you. And if they are not joined to you, you can't make them stay. Let them go. And it doesn't mean that they are a bad person; it just means that their part in the story is over. And you've got to know when people's part in your story is over, so that you don't keep trying to raise the dead.

You've got to know when it's dead.
You've got to know when it's over.
I've got the gift of goodbye.
It's the tenth spiritual gift. I believe in goodbye.
It's not that I'm hateful, it's that I'm faithful, and I know whatever God means for me to have, He'll give it to me.

And if it takes too much sweat I don't need it. Stop begging people to stay. LET THEM GO!

If you are holding on to something that doesn't belong to you and was never intended for your life, then you need to - LET IT GO!

If you are holding on to past hurts and pains  - LET THEM GO!

If someone can't treat you right, love you back, and see your worth - LET THEM GO!

If someone has angered you - LET THEM GO!

If you are holding on to thoughts of evil and revenge - LET THEM GO!

If you are involved in a wrong relationship or addiction - LET IT GO!

If you are holding on to a job that no longer meets your needs or talents - LET IT GO!

If you have a bad attitude - LET IT GO!

If you keep judging others to make yourself feel better - LET IT GO!

If you're stuck in the past and God is trying to take you to a new level in Him - LET IT GO!

If you are struggling with the healing of a broken relationship - LET IT GO!

If you keep trying to help someone who won't even try to help themselves – LET THEM GO!

If you're feeling depressed and stressed  - LET IT GO!

If there is a particular situation that you are so used to handling yourself and God is saying "take your hands off of it," then you need to - LET IT GO!

Let the past be the past. Forget the former things. GOD is doing a new thing for YOU!

LET IT GO!

Get right or get left think about it, and then LET IT GO!

*T. D. Jakes* (modified)

# GOD'S BOXES

I have in my hands two boxes,
Which God gave me to hold.
He said, "Put all your sorrows in the black box,
And all your joys in the gold."

I heeded His words, and in the two boxes,
Both my joys and sorrows I stored,
But though the gold became heavier each day,
The black was as light as before.

With curiosity, I opened the black box,
I wanted to find out why,
And I saw, in the base of the box, a hole,
Which my sorrows had fallen out by.

I showed the hole to God, and mused,
"I wonder where my sorrows could be!"
He smiled a gentle smile and said,
"My child, they're all here with me."

I asked God, why He gave me the boxes,
Why the gold and the black with the hole?
"My child, the gold is for you to count your
blessings,
The black is for you to let go."

# WHEN I SAY...

When I say, "I'm a Christian"
I am not shouting, "I am saved"
I'm whispering, "I was lost"
That's why I chose this way.

When I say, "I'm a Christian"
I don't speak of this with pride.
I'm confessing that I stumble
And need someone to be my guide.

When I say, "I'm a Christian"
I'm not trying to be strong.
I'm professing that I am weak
And pray for strength to carry on.

When I say, "I'm a Christian"
I'm not bragging of success.
I'm admitting that I've failed
And can't ever pay the debt.

When I say, "I'm a Christian"
I'm not claiming to be perfect,
My flaws are too visible
But God believes I'm worth it.

When I say, "I'm a Christian"
I still feel the sting of pain;
I have my share of heartaches
Which is why I speak His name.

# A WISH FOR YOU

May there always be work for your hands to do,
May your purse always hold a coin or two.

May the sun always shine on your windowpane,
May a rainbow be certain to follow each rain.

May the hand of a friend always be near you,
May God fill your heart with gladness to cheer
you.

# GOD IS ALWAYS THERE

Whatever your cross,
Whatever your pain
There will always be sunshine
After the rain.

Perhaps you may stumble,
Perhaps even fall,
But God's always there
          To help you through it all.

# TODAY

Today, I will delete from my diary two days: yesterday and tomorrow.

Yesterday was to learn and tomorrow will be the consequence of what I do today.

Today, I will face life with the conviction that this day will not ever return.

Today, I will be brave enough not to let opportunities pass me by, my only alternative is to succeed.

Today, I will invest my most valuable resource: my time, in the most transcendental work: my life. I will spend each minute passionately to make of today a different and unique day in my life.

Today I will defy every obstacle that appears in my way, trusting I will succeed.

Today I will resist pessimism and will conquer the world with a smile, with the positive attitude of expecting always the best.

Today I will take the time to be happy and will leave my footprints in the hearts of others.

# A SMILE

Smiling is infectious;
You catch it like the flu,
When someone smiled at me today
I started smiling too.
I passed around the corner
And someone saw my grin,
When he smiled I realised
I'd passed it on to him.

I thought about that smile
Then I realised its worth,
A single smile, just like mine
Could travel round the earth.
So, if you feel a smile begin,
Don't leave it undetected
Let's start an epidemic quick,
And get the world infected!

# THE PASSION

As I stood outside the doors;
I tried to prepare myself
For what I was about to see.
But when I entered the room
I had no idea that my life would be
changed so drastically.

I sat there in silence, as all did.
The room was filled with the flickering
light of the screen.
As I cried, only a little bit, too shocked to move,
I felt like my heart was broken inside me.
I wanted to cry more, but felt it hard to breathe
I watched in silence,
As this man demonstrated what Jesus did for
me.

It broke my heart and tears began to flow.
I felt helpless and I wanted to make them stop.
The pain I felt was like nothing I've ever felt
before.
Then I began to cry out to God.
I realised at that moment if He had not done this
for me,
This love that I feel for Him now would have
never come to be.

He laid in the temple yard beaten His face
disfigured from the punches and blows.

The robe he wore was covered in blood as red as
a rose.
With every ounce of His strength He pulled
himself to His feet.
Only to be knocked down again.
But all that He did was for me. What greater love
shown by a friend?

When they lead Him away, His body was
weakened by the pain.
The Roman soldiers had no pity on Him and
began to beat Him again.
They slapped Him in the face and knocked Him
to the ground.
No idea that this was all for them as well.
That this man would one day rise up and reign
over all man and save many from Hell.

As He carried the cross on His back to the place
where He would soon die,
You could hear people weeping all over the
room,
As many in the crowd cried.
We all knew what was next and it made it hard
to bear.
All our eyes were fixed on the screen.
All you could hear was the sobbing cries of the
weeping;
The sounds of those mourning in despair.

The actor lay on the cross as they drove the nails
in his hands and in his feet.

But I could see only Jesus there, giving His life
for me.
The movie became real, the pain was real, the
tears and the blood.
And then it was like God spoke to me and said,
"There is no greater love. My son did this for you.
He laid his life down so you wouldn't have to.
He traded his crown in Heaven for a crown of
thorns and a beating you would never endure."

I knew at that moment that this had to be.
Even though it seemed so unfair.
But the greatest thing happened! God caused
my eyes to open and see,
The crucifixion became clear.
I could truly see what really happened.
No greater love was shown to me,
Than the day Christ was nailed to that tree.

*Patricia Montgomery*

# I ASKED GOD

I asked for a flower,
He gave me a garden.
I asked for a tree,
He gave me a forest.
I asked for a river,
He gave me an ocean.
I asked God for life,
He sent Jesus to die so I could have eternal
life

Thank you Jesus.

# WORDS TO LIVE BY

# RESUME

NAME: GOD

ADDRESS: Everywhere (Omnipresent)
PHONE: 0800 4U2 - PRAY

EXPERIENCE:
From before the beginning of time.
From everlasting to everlasting  (I made time).

ABILITY:
All powerful (Omnipotent).

PRIOR EMPLOYMENT:
Created the universe; put the galaxies in place;
formed man.
Established Heaven and Earth by My spoken
word and am currently holding the world and
universe together by My sole power.

EDUCATION AND TRAINING:
I am - I am all Knowledge; I am Truth; I am Light.
I am understanding; I am Life; I am The Way. I
am the good shepherd. I and the Father are One.
(Omniscient).

CHARACTER REFERENCE:
Love, light and life (1 John 4:16, 1 John 1:5,
John 14:6).
A representative, but by no means conclusive,
list of other character traits follows:
Wisdom - James 1:5
Comfort - 2 Corinthians 1:3

Truth - John 8:32
Healer - 1 Peter 2:24
Strength - Phil. 4:13
Forgiveness - 1 John 1:9
Provider - Phil. 4:19
Mercy - Ephesians 2:24
Good - Matt. 19:17
Peace - Romans 14:17

AVAILABILITY:
I am willing and ready to take over your life at a
moments notice; able to provide you with
salvation and everlasting life. I will bring all of
who I am into your life. I can start immediately.
I am available for 24 hours a day
companionship, counselling, guidance, comfort
and consolation; to strengthen you and stand
with you against all attacks from the enemy; to
renew your mind and spirit, and to transform you
into a creature if you let Me. I will become your
life and you will become My body.

SALARY REQUIREMENT:
Payment for all work that has and will be
accomplished in your life, has already been paid
through the blood of My Son.

YOUR RESPONSIBILITY:
Your only responsibility is to believe and commit,
to have faith, and trust and obey what Jesus has
done and wants to do in your life. I look forward
to meeting you personally.

# SIXTEEN WISE SAYINGS

1. The best way to get even is to forget.

2. Feed your faith and your doubts will starve to death.

3. Some marriages are made in heaven, but they all have to be maintained on earth.

4. A successful marriage isn't finding the right person; it's being the right person.

5. Unless you can create the whole universe in five days, then perhaps giving advice to God isn't such a good idea.

6. Sorrow looks back, worry looks around, and faith looks up.

7. Standing in the middle of the road is dangerous. The traffic from both sides will knock you down.

8. Words are windows to the heart.

9. A sceptic is a person who, when he sees the handwriting on the wall, claims it's forgery.

10. The mighty oak tree was once a little nut that held its ground.

11. Too many people offer God prayers with claw marks all over them.

12. The tongue must be heavy indeed, because so few people can hold it.

13. To forgive is to set the prisoner free, and then discover the prisoner was you.

14. You'll notice that a turtle only makes progress when it sticks out its neck.

15. If the grass is greener on the other side of the fence, you can bet the water bill is higher.

16. Don't play God – there is only one!

# A STATE OF MIND

If you think you are beaten,
You are.
If you think you dare not,
You don't.

If you'd like to win but think you'll lose,
You're lost.

For out in the world we find,
Success begins with a person's faith.
It's all in the state of mind.

Life's battles don't always go
To the stronger or faster hand.
They go to the one who trusts in God
And always thinks... I CAN.

# DON'T SPEND MAJOR TIME WITH MINOR PEOPLE.

If there are people in your life who continually disappoint you, break promises, stomp on your dreams, are too judgmental, and don't have your back during difficult times, they are not friends.

To have a friend you have to be a friend. In life, as you grow, your friends will either grow or go. Surround yourself with people who have high values, goals, interests and a clean lifestyle.

When I think of any of my successes, I am thankful to God from whom all blessings flow, and to my family and friends who enrich my life.

Over the years, my phone book has changed because I changed for the better.

At first you think you are going to be alone, but after a while new people show up in your life and make your life so much sweeter and easier to endure.

Remember what your elders used to say, "Birds of the same feather always stay together." If you're an eagle, don't hang around chickens because chickens can't fly!

Yes, I do love Jesus. He is the source of my existence and my Saviour. He keeps me functioning each and every day.

Without Him, I will be nothing.
Without Him, I am nothing.
With Him I can do all things.

Be positive. Be progressive. Take the time to make a positive difference in someone's life.

# LIFE'S ABC

A - Accept
Accept others for who they are and for the choices they have made, even if you have difficulty understanding their beliefs, motives or actions.

B - Break Away
Break away from everything that stands in the way of what you hope to accomplish with your life.

C - Create
Create a family of friends whom you can share your hopes, dreams, sorrows and happiness with.

D - Decide
Decide that you'll be successful and happy come what may, and good things will find you. The roadblocks are only minor obstacles along the way.

E - Explore
Explore and experiment. The world has much to offer, and you have much to give. And every time you try something new, you will learn more about yourself.

F - Forgive
Forgive and encourage. Grudges only weigh you down and inspire unhappiness and grief.

Soar above it, and remember that everyone makes mistakes.

**G - Grow**
Leave the childhood monsters behind. They can no longer hurt you or stand in your way.

**H - Hope**
Hope for the best and never forget that anything is possible as long as you remain dedicated to the task.

**I - Ignore**
Ignore the negative voice inside your head. Focus instead on your goals and remember your accomplishments. Your past success is only a small inkling of what the future holds.

**J - Journey**
Journey to new worlds and new possibilities by remaining open-minded. Try to learn something new every day, and you will grow.

**K - Know**
Know that no matter how bad things seem, they'll always get better. The warmth of spring always follows the harshest winter.

**L - Love**
Let love fill your heart instead of hate. When hate is in your heart, there's room for nothing else; but when love is in your heart, there's room for endless happiness.

**M** - Manage
Manage your time and your expenses wisely,
and you will suffer from less stress and worry.
Then you will be able to focus on the important
things in life.

**N** - Notice
Never ignore the poor, infirm, helpless, weak or
suffering. Offer your assistance when possible,
and always your kindness and understanding.

**O** - Open
Open your eyes and take in all the beauty
around you. Even during the worst of times,
there is still much to be thankful for.

**P** - Play
Never forget to have fun along the way. Success
means nothing without happiness.

**Q** - Question
Ask many questions, because you are here to
learn.

**R** - Relax
Refuse to let worry and stress rule your life, and
remember that things always have a way of
working out in the end.

**S - Share**
Share your talent, skills, knowledge and time
with others. Everything that you invest in others
will return to you many times over.

**T - Try**
Even when your dreams seem impossible to
reach, try anyway. You'll be amazed by what you
can accomplish.

**U - Use**
Use your gifts to your best ability. Talent that's
wasted has no value. Talent that's used will
bring unexpected rewards.

**V - Value**
Value the friends and family members who've
supported and encouraged you, and be there for
them as well.

**W - Work**
Work hard every day to be the best person you
know.

**X - Xerox**
Xerox every good value and character and
distribute it among your friends. They will think
you are a genius.

**Y - Yearn**
Yearn for better, and better will come.

**Z - Zealous**
Be zealous for Christ, and He will reward you
bountifully.

# A PURPOSE TO LIFE'S EVENTS

When you feel down because you didn't get what you wanted, just sit tight and be happy, because God has thought of something better to give you.

When something happens to you, good or bad, consider what it means. There's a purpose to life's events: to teach you how to laugh more or not to cry too hard.

You can't make someone love you. All you can do is be someone who can be loved; the rest is up to the person to realize your worth.

It's better to lose your pride to the one you love, than to lose the one you love because of pride.

We spend too much time looking for the right person to love or finding fault with those we already love, when instead we should be perfecting the love we give.

Never abandon an old friend. You will never find one who can take his or her place.


IN EVERYTHING GIVE THANKS TO GOD

# GOD'S ROAD SIGNS

New billboards are getting attention in Arizona. Some reported seeing one or two messages, but the newspaper listed all of them.
Here's a list of all variations of the "God Speaks" billboards. The billboards are a simple black background with white text. No fine print or sponsoring organization is included. These are awesome...enjoy.

Tell the kids I love them.
-God

Let's meet at my house, say once a week.
-God

C'mon over and bring the kids.
-God

What part of "Thou Shalt Not" didn't you understand?
-God

We need to talk.
-God

Keep using my name in vain, I'll make rush hour longer.
-God

Loved the wedding, invite me to the marriage.

-God

That "Love Thy Neighbour" thing...I meant it.
-God

I love you and you and you and you and...
-God

Will the road you're on get you to my place?
-God

Follow me.
-God

Big bang theory, you've got to be kidding?
-God

My way is the highway.
-God

Need directions?
-God

Have you read my No.1 best seller? There will be a test.
-God

Do you have any idea where you're going?
-God

Don't make me come down there.
-God

# VACANCIES

The Kingdom of God is hiring! Are you ready to apply? Do you qualify?

JOB TITLE: Disciples for Christ

JOB DESCRIPTION: Tell the dying world how to live through Jesus Christ

NUMBER OF AVAILABLE POSITIONS: Unlimited. Everyone is welcome: preachers, teachers, singers, musicians, missionaries, guardians, food servers, and numerous others that we just can't list them all here

EXCEPTION TO AVAILABLE POSITIONS: The vacancy of Boss has already been filled by the Holy Spirit

QUALIFICATIONS: Must have previously sinned and been blood washed; must be willing to press toward the mark of the high calling in Christ Jesus

EXPERIENCE NEEDED: None necessary; experience will be earned through on-the-job training

EDUCATION: The Holy Spirit will teach you all things

BENEFIT PACKAGE/SALARY: God (the employer) shall supply all your needs according to His riches in glory

INSURANCE: Access to the Master Physician

PACKAGE ALSO INCLUDES: Love, joy, peace, patience, long suffering; Lawyer, Comforter, and a Wonderful Counsellor

RECOMPENSE FOR COMPLETING THE JOB ASSIGNMENT: The most important benefit: eternal life with the employer.

DEADLINE FOR APPLICATIONS: Before the return of Jesus Christ; date/hour not known; wise to apply *today*

IMPORTANT WARNING: Satan and his demons need not apply

# ROAD TO SUCCESS

The road to success is not straight. There is a curve called *failure*. A loop called *confusion*, speed bumps called *friends*, red lights called *enemies*, caution lights called *family*. You will have flats called *jobs*.

But, if you have a spare called *determination*, an engine called *perseverance*, insurance called *faith*, a driver called *Jesus*, you will make it to a place called *success*!

***

If God had a refrigerator, your picture would be on it.

If he had a wallet, your photo would be in it.

# MY GARDEN

For the garden of your daily living...

Plant three rows of peas:
1. Peace of mind
2. Peace of heart
3. Peace of soul

Plant four rows of squash:
1. Squash gossip
2. Squash indifference
3. Squash grumbling
4. Squash selfishness

Plant four rows of lettuce:
1. Lettuce be faithful
2. Lettuce be kind
3. Lettuce be patient
4. Lettuce really love one another

No garden is without turnips:
1. Turnip for meetings
2. Turnip for service
3. Turnip to help one another

To conclude our garden we must have thyme:
1. Thyme for each other
2. Thyme for family
3. Thyme for friends

Water freely with patience and cultivate with love. There is fruit in your garden because you reap what you sow.

# MOVING THOUGHTS

Maybe God wants us to meet a few wrong people before meeting the right one, so that when we finally meet the right person, we will know how to be grateful for that gift.

When the door of happiness closes, another opens. But often times we look so long at the closed door that we don't see the one that has been opened for us.

It is true that we don't know what we've got until we lose it, but it is also true that we don't know what we've been missing until it arrives.

Giving someone all your love is never an assurance that they will love you back! Don't expect love in return; just wait for it to grow in their heart. And if it doesn't, be content that it grew in yours.

It takes only a minute to get a 'crush' on someone, an hour to like someone, and a day to love someone; but it takes a lifetime to forget someone.

Don't go for looks; they can deceive. Don't go for wealth; even that fades away. Go for someone who makes you happy, someone who makes your heart smile, because it takes only a smile to make a dark day seem bright.

There are moments in life when you miss someone so much that you just want to pick them from your dreams and hug them for real!

Dream what you want to dream, go where you want to go, be what you want to be, because you have only one life and one chance to do all the things you want to do.

Always put yourself in others' shoes. If you feel that it hurts you, it probably hurts the other person too.

The happiest of people don't necessarily have the best of everything; they just make the most of things that come along their way.

Happiness lives for those who cry, those who hurt, those who have searched, and those who have tried; for only they can appreciate the importance of people who have touched their lives.

Love begins with a smile, grows with a kiss and ends with a tear.

The brightest future will always be based on a forgotten past. You can't go on well in life until you let go of your past failures and heartaches.

When you were born, you were crying and everyone around you was smiling. Live your life so that when you die, you are the one who is smiling and everyone around you is crying.

# THE MOST...

The most destructive habit - worry
The greatest joy - giving
The greatest loss - loss of self-respect
The most satisfying work - helping others
The ugliest personality trait - selfishness

The most endangered species - dedicated
leaders
The greatest 'shot in the arm' - encouragement
The greatest problem to overcome - fear
The most effective sleeping pill - peace of mind
The most crippling failure disease - excuses
The most powerful force in life - love

The most dangerous pariah - a gossiper
The world's most incredible computer - the brain
The worst thing to be without - hope
The deadliest weapon - the tongue
The two most power-filled words - 'I can'
The greatest asset - faith

The most worthless emotion - self-pity
The most beautiful attire - a smile
The most prized possession - integrity
The most powerful channel of communication -
prayer
The most contagious spirit – enthusiasm

# FROM AMERICA

DID YOU KNOW?
As you walk up the steps in front of the U.S. Supreme Court building, you can see near the top of the facade a row of figures representing the world's lawgivers. Each one is facing the one in the middle, who is facing forward with a full frontal view. That figure is of Moses and he is holding the Ten Commandments.

DID YOU KNOW?
As you enter the Supreme Court courtroom, the two huge oak doors of the portal have the Ten Commandments engraved on the lower portion of each door.

DID YOU KNOW?
As you sit inside the courtroom, plainly visible on the rear wall, right above where the Supreme Court judges sit, is a display of the Ten Commandments.

DID YOU KNOW?
There are Bible verses etched in stone all over the Federal Buildings and Monuments in Washington, D.C.

DID YOU KNOW?
James Madison, the fourth president, known as "The Father of Our Constitution" made the following statement: "We have staked the whole of all our political institutions upon the capacity of mankind for self-government, upon the

capacity of each and all of us to govern ourselves, to control ourselves, to sustain ourselves, according to the Ten Commandments of God."

DID YOU KNOW?
Patrick Henry, the patriot considered one of the Founding Fathers of the USA, famous for the quote, "Give me liberty or give me death," also said, "It cannot be emphasised too strongly or too often that this great nation was founded not by religionists but by Christians, not on religions but on the Gospel of Jesus Christ."

DID YOU KNOW?
Every session of Congress begins with a prayer by a paid preacher, whose salary has been paid by the taxpayer since 1777.

DID YOU KNOW?
Fifty-two of the 55 founders of the Constitution were members of the established orthodox churches in the colonies.

DID YOU KNOW?
Thomas Jefferson worried that the Courts would overstep their authority and instead of interpreting the law would begin making law an oligarchy, the rule of few over many.

DID YOU KNOW?
The very first Supreme Court Justice, John Jay, said, "Americans should select and prefer Christians as their rulers."

# THINK ABOUT IT

Have you ever wondered which hurts the most: saying something and wishing you hadn't, or saying nothing and wishing you had?

I suppose the most important things are the hardest things to say.

Don't be afraid to tell someone you love them. If you do, they might break your heart. If you don't, you might break theirs.

Too many of us stay walled up because we are afraid to care too much, for fear that the other person does not care as much, or even at all.

Have you ever denied your feelings for someone because your fear of rejection was too hard to handle?

We tell lies when we are afraid; afraid of what we don't know; afraid of what others will think; afraid of what will be found out about us. But every time we tell a lie, the thing we fear grows stronger.

Life is all about risks and it requires you to jump.

Anger is a condition in which the tongue works faster than the mind.

All people smile in the same language.

The real measure of a man's wealth is what he has invested in eternity.

Laughter is God's sunshine. If you fill your heart with regrets of yesterday and the worries of tomorrow, you have no today to be thankful for.

If anyone speaks badly of you, live so none will believe it.

The best thing parents can do for their children is to love each other.

Harsh words break no bones but they do break hearts. For every minute you are angry with someone, you lose 60 seconds of happiness that you can never get back.

Do what you can, for whom you can, with what you have, and where you are.

# THINGS GOD WON'T ASK

God won't ask what kind of car you drove; He'll ask how many people you carried who didn't have transportation.

God won't ask the square footage of your house; He'll ask how many people you welcomed into your home.

God won't ask about the clothes you had in your closet; He'll ask how many you helped to clothe.

God won't ask what your highest salary was; He'll ask if you compromised your character to obtain it.

God won't ask what your job title was; He'll ask if you performed your job to the best of your ability.

God won't ask how many friends you had; He'll ask how many people to whom you were a friend.

God won't ask in what neighbourhood you lived; He'll ask how you treated your neighbours.

God won't ask about the colour of your skin; He'll ask about the content of your character.

God won't ask why it took you so long to seek salvation; He'll lovingly welcome you to your mansion in heaven.

# THIRTY-EIGHT GEMS TO LIVE BY

1. Pray

2. Go to bed on time.

3. Get up on time so you can start the day unrushed.

4. Say No to projects that won't fit into your time schedule or that will compromise your mental health.

5. Delegate tasks to capable others.

6. Simplify and unclutter your life.

7. Less is more. (Although one is often not enough, two is often too many.)

8. Allow extra time to do things and to get to places.

9. Pace yourself. Spread out big changes and difficult projects over time; don't lump the hard things all together.

10. Take one day at a time.

11. Separate worries from concerns. If a situation is a concern, find out what God would

have you to do and let go of the anxiety. If you can't do anything about a situation, forget it.

12. Live within your budget.

13. Have backups: an extra car key in your wallet, an extra house key buried in the garden, extra stamps, etc.,

14. K.M.S. (Keep Mouth Shut). This single piece of advice can prevent an enormous amount of trouble.

15. Do something for the kid in you everyday.

16. Carry a Bible with you to read while waiting in line.

17. Get enough exercise.

18. Eat right.

19. Get organised so everything has its place.

20. Listen to a tape while driving that can help improve your quality of life.

21. Write thoughts and inspirations down.

22. Every day, find time to be alone.

23. Having problems? Talk to God on the spot. Try to nip small problems in the bud. Don't wait until it's time to go to bed to try and pray.

24. Make friends with godly people.

25. Keep a folder of favourite scriptures on hand.

26. Remember that the shortest bridge between despair and hope is often a good "Thank you, Jesus!"

30. Develop a forgiving attitude (most people are doing the best they can).

31. Be kind to unkind people (they probably need it the most).

32. Sit on your ego.

33. Talk less, listen more.

35. Remind yourself that you are not the managing director of the universe.

36. Every night before bed, think of one thing you're grateful for that you've never been grateful for before.

37. Just remember: To the world you might be one person, but to one person you just might be the world.

38. Know from where you came. If you know from where you came, there are absolutely no limitations to where you can go

GOD HAS A WAY OF TURNING THINGS AROUND FOR YOU.

"If God is for us, who can be against us?" (Romans 8:31)

# GOD IS THERE

Have you ever been just sitting there, and all of a sudden you feel like doing something nice for someone you care for? That's God talking to you through the Holy Spirit..

Have you ever been down and out and nobody seems to be around for you to talk to? That's God wanting you to talk to Him.

Have you ever been thinking about somebody that you haven't seen in a long time and then next thing you know you see them or receive a phone call from them? That's God. There is no such thing as coincidence.

Have you ever received something wonderful that you didn't even ask for, like money in the post, a debt that mysteriously has been cleared, or a coupon to a department store where you had just seen something you needed, but couldn't afford? That's God knowing the desires of your heart.

Have you ever been in a situation and you had no clue how it was going to get better, how the hurting would stop, how the pain would ease, but now you can look back on it. That's God passing you through tribulation to see a brighter day.

# MIRACLE AND MYSTERY

In the tiny petal of a tiny flower
That grew from a tiny pod,
Is the miracle and the mystery
Of all creation and God!

# CIRCLE OF FRIENDS

A ball is a circle, no beginning and no end.
It keeps us together like our circle of friends.
But the treasure inside for you to see,
Is the treasure of friendship you've granted to
me.

*  *  *

Coincidence is when God chooses to remain
anonymous.

# OTHER BOOKS BY MANDRA PUBLISHING

GOD.COM (first volume). Inspirational and encouraging. "Full of pearl drops of wisdom encased in clouds of light humour." It will certainly make you smile, whatever your culture or background. You will want your friends to read it. *Cost: £5.95*

GOD.COM 2. This is the book in your hand. *Cost: £6.50*
Are you waiting for volume 3?

Let the Earth Speak of God's Creation (Illustrated).
A fresh look at the creation argument, with a good balance between science and Scripture; new info. on dinosaurs. Valuable to anyone with GCSE and above education. *Chapters include*: Origin and Structure of the Earth, Up and Down the Geological Column, Extraterrestrial Impact, Cool Running, Taming the T-Rex, The Geological Column and Calvary. *Cost: £6.50*

Spiritual Gifts: Identify and Develop Them (Revised). The first edition sold out. It lives up to its title, providing scriptural basis for the identification and development of one's spiritual gifts; and helps the reader to examine new gifts, while facilitating creativity in developing them.

*Chapters Include*: The Basic Principle, Definition and Application, Implication and Action, Evidence in your Life, *Cost: £5.95*

**Sanctified Weakness** is more than a collection of inspirational sermons speaking to the heart and mind of young people, or anyone. It is also the story of a life, weak in the flesh, but touched by God. You won't be able to put it down. Chapters include: Chasing Bubbles, Giant Killer, Can't Cook, Won't Cook – Death in the Pot, Keeping it Real, Get a Life, Dream On. *Cost: £5.95*

Please see our website for other titles that are pending.

www.mandrapublishing.com

# ORDERS

You may obtain any of our books through various convenient outlets, or send your order with a cheque to:

*Mandra Publishing,*
*PO Box 5136*
*Riseley*
*RG7 1GT*
*UK*

**Postage & Packing** (UK only): For one book please add £1.50 and for two books add £2.50.

> P&P is **free** for 3 or more books.

> **Clients outside the UK** should contact us for the relevant P&P charges.

**Discount:** You may wish to ask for a discount for orders over 10 books.

**Commercial:** Bookshops, distributors and other commercial outlets, please contact us for our favourable terms.

**Contact:**

> Tel:  0118 9882 880
> +44 (0) 118 9882 880
> E-mail: Mandra0714@aol.com
> www.mandrapublishing.com